ISLE OF MAN

RIDER'S GUIDE

ISLE OF MAN

RIDER'S GUIDE

RAY KNIGHT

Published in 1991 by Osprey Publishing,
59 Grosvenor Street, London W1X 9DA

British Library Cataloguing in Publication Data

Knight, Ray
    TT rider's guide.
    1. Isle of Man. Racetracks: Tourist Trophy
    mountain course. Racing motorcycles. Racing
    I. Title
    796.75094279
ISBN 1-85532-117-3

Editor Ian Penberthy
Page design Gwyn Lewis

Phototypeset and printed in Great Britain by
BAS Printers Limited, Over Wallop, Hampshire

Contents

About the author

Journalist Ray Knight has a TT win, 17 Replicas, some 80 races and over 25,000 miles on the Isle of Man mountain course to his credit. In *TT Rider's Guide*, he has set down his experience for the benefit of both intending competitors and those who visit the Island at race times to be part of this unique motorcycling experience.

He first rode on the mountain circuit in the 1962 Senior Manx Grand Prix on a home-built machine, based on an AJS 7R rolling chassis and a Royal Enfield twin motor. After stopping on the last lap to recover from being soaked through and frozen stiff, he finished in 56th place.

His first ride in the TT came in 1967, when production races were introduced and, to date (1990), he has entered this event every year since.

In 1968 he won the 500 cc Production TT Race on a Triumph Daytona, setting lap and race records that stood for three years. He finished second, third and fourth in succeeding years.

In a racing career spanning 30 years, Ray has competed at international level, taken part in endurance grands prix, won many club championships, and been a race machine tester and reporter for *Motorcyclist Illustrated*, *Road Racing* and *Motorcycle Sport* magazines. He has ridden factory-supported Royal Enfield, Norton, Ducati, BMW and Triumph motorcycles.

Finally, at the ripe old age of 55, he achieved a production machine lap in the TT that was just short of 110 mph on his own 1100 GSXR-R Suzuki, and 105 mph on a private 600 CBR Honda.

Dedication

This book is dedicated to all of the riders who have raced in the Isle of Man, and to their mechanics and faithful supporters. They, and the countless unpaid workers who are part of the organization, have all contributed to making the Isle of Man a legend in motorcycle sport.

In researching this book, I should like to thank Peter Kneale of the TT Press Office for his help and permission to quote from *TT Talk*.

Introduction

There is a certain magic associated with the Isle of Man, if you happen to be a motorcyclist. 'The Island' was once Britain's greatest circuit – where the Grand Prix was held – and if you are an enthusiast for real road racing, it probably still is the greatest. But then the Isle of Man is so much more than just the races; there are rallies, sprints, club meetings, glorious scenery, the camaraderie of tens of thousands of like-minded enthusiasts, and a ready welcome for the motorcyclist.

Racing around 37.7 miles of public roads on every lap approaches a science for the rider, and it provides the knowledgeable enthusiast with a fascinating and satisfying involvement in a unique spectacle.

This book is my attempt at the impossible: to guide the novice rider through the Island's 264 bends – and to convey to the spectator an awareness of the magnitude of the task the course represents for those lucky enough to be able to try. Hopefully, it will generate added involvement and enjoyment for the enthusiasts who keep the TT alive.

I have covered more than the races over the mountain circuit, for also detailed are the *other races* – on the Billown circuit, and Jurby and Andreas – together with the history of them all.

Ray Knight

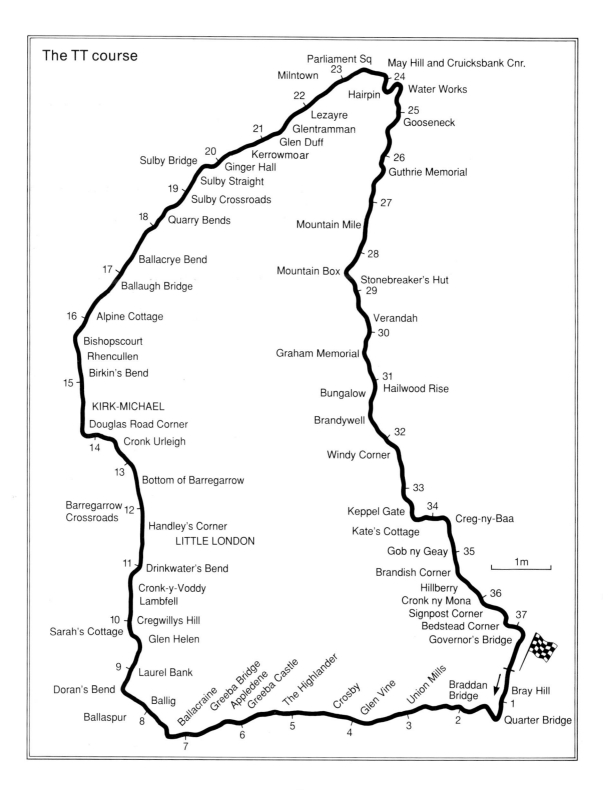

The TT course

Parliament Sq
23
Milntown
22
Lezayre
21
Glentramman
Glen Duff
20
Kerrowmoar
Sulby Bridge
Ginger Hall
Sulby Straight
19
Sulby Crossroads
18
Quarry Bends

Ballacrye Bend
17
Ballaugh Bridge

16
Alpine Cottage

Bishopscourt
Rhencullen
Birkin's Bend
15

KIRK-MICHAEL
Douglas Road Corner
Cronk Urleigh
14
13
Bottom of Barregarrow
Barregarrow 12
Crossroads
Handley's Corner
LITTLE LONDON

11
Drinkwater's Bend
Cronk-y-Voddy
Lambfell
10
Cregwillys Hill
Sarah's Cottage
Glen Helen

9
Laurel Bank
Doran's Bend
Ballig
Ballaspur
8

Hairpin

May Hill and Cruicksbank Cnr.
24
Water Works
25
Gooseneck
26
Guthrie Memorial
27
Mountain Mile
28
Mountain Box
Stonebreaker's Hut
29
Verandah
30
Graham Memorial
31
Hailwood Rise
Bungalow
Brandywell
32
Windy Corner
33
Keppel Gate 34
Kate's Cottage Creg-ny-Baa
Gob ny Geay 35
1m
Brandish Corner
Hillberry
Cronk ny Mona 36
Signpost Corner
Bedstead Corner 37
Governor's Bridge

Ballacraine
Greeba Bridge
Appledene
Greeba Castle
The Highlander
Crosby
Glen Vine
Union Mills
Braddan
Bridge
Bray Hill
1
Quarter Bridge
2
3
4
5
6
7

8

1 The Island scene - biker's paradise

For 14 days every June, the Isle of Man becomes a veritable biker's paradise with the running of the TT, while the Manx Grand Prix, held in September, has its own special atmosphere, too.

The one major aspect that sets the Isle of Man apart from other places the motorcycle enthusiast may visit is simply that the atmosphere is not that of toleration, but more of welcome. It may be enlightened self-interest in an Island still heavily committed to the tourist trade, but it is a fact that the motorcyclist is welcome – and leathers are not a problem in the foyers of the Island's hotels.

On joining the crowds of bikes and racers' vans at either Liverpool or Heysham, you will become part of a scene that must be close to motorcyclists' heaven. Around 50,000 like-minded enthusiasts will be heading for an Island devoted to serving their interests for the following couple of weeks while the TT is run.

The Manx Grand Prix fortnight will attract a hardcore of, say, 400 competitors, plus their families and supporters, and a surprising number of dedicated enthusiasts. It generates quite a different atmosphere to the TT. Indeed, away from the circuit, you would hardly know that the biggest thing in club racing was taking place. It is an excellent opportunity for a holiday that takes in a modicum of biking and a lot of what the Island has to offer as an attractive holiday venue with a variety of scenery that is hard to match anywhere in the British Isles.

500 miles of fun

There are some 500 miles of roads within the 227 square miles of this small island, and no speed limit outside the towns and villages. They provide a chance to open up a bike over the mountain, or enjoy the myriad country lanes and a wide variety of going.

For the road rider, half the fun of the holiday will be simply exploring all those roads and lanes with the aid of an Ordnance Survey map. For green laners, it should be remembered that, in earlier years, the Island has been the venue of the International Six Days Trial. There are tests for the well-mounted expert as well as easier going for the less experienced on a modern roadster enduro bike.

A few routes number among my own particular favourites and must not be missed. Among these is the Marine Drive through to Port Soderick. Unfortunately, there has been a landslip halfway along it and the road has been closed to motor transport, and it does not look like being repaired. However, you can walk through, which is well worth the effort, as the views are breathtaking.

No visit would be complete without riding out through Castletown and on to the point to see the Calf of Man. From there, it is a short ride to Port Erin; the route up the Sloc road, keeping close to the coast by the Round Table, is one of the most beautiful that I know in the Island. Turning left and passing through Dalby, Glen Maye and on to Peel will complete a truly worthwhile excursion.

After sampling the delights of Peel – and the castle is worth spending some time at – continue along the coast road to Knocksharry, through Glenmoar and join the TT circuit at Kirk Michael.

A visit to The Ayres Manx Conservation will provide a considerable change of scenery that is difficult to believe in such a small island. The northern part of the Island is flat and presents quite a different character with its long beach. It can be reached by taking any of the lanes leading off the course after Rhencullin – a good spectating spot – or by following the Bride coast road out of Ramsey.

Going the other way out of Ramsey, take the Port-e-Vullen road towards Maughold Head, through Ballajora, on to Ballaglass Glen and then to Glen Mona. This one will show you some superb residences and delightful country lanes.

There is plenty to interest the steam buff in the Isle of Man. 'Hutchinson', seen here, is one of the engines that run from Douglas to Port Erin

Of course, there are many other runs that should not be missed, and the map will show enough lanes to keep you busy for a fortnight when not attending rallies or watching races. A recent feature that is most useful is the TT Access Road. This allows access to the inside of the circuit, from the outside, during races.

The Access Road actually runs from the Quarter Bridge-Castletown Road, the entrance being just short of the bridge, so you have to skirt round the course to reach it. Following the usual road out of Douglas from the Quay, turn left through the industrial estate, as you will find most other traffic doing during the races, then turn right, back to

ABOVE LEFT

There is an abundance of glorious scenery in the Isle of Man; this is the view over the Calf of Man, a place for seabirds and seals

LEFT

The magnificent Peel Castle is a must for anyone with an interest in the Island's history. It is the current scene of an archaeological dig, revealing hundreds of years of the Island's history

Quarter Bridge. The road is laid over the old railway line and passes under Braddon Bridge, then up through the housing estate and on to almost anywhere inside the circuit: Baldwin – Injebreck Reservoir, Barregarrow, Cronk-y-Voddy – Ballaugh, Brandywell, Cronk-ny-Mona and St Ninian's crossroads.

Another fun ride is around Sulby Reservoir after spectating at Sulby crossroads or Ginger Hall – a good 'jar' is to be had at both.

Railways

There are three 'musts' for anyone with even the slightest of interests in railways: the Douglas-Peel Victorian steam line (the terminal is by the Quay in Douglas); the Douglas-Laxey-Ramsey electric line; and the one of real interest to race fans, the branch line of the electric railway from Laxey up to Snaefell where, at the Bungalow, a good day's spectating may be had – on a nice day, that is.

There is yet another railway that is well worth a visit. They have just restored most of the old line out around the Head at Groudle Glen. This is reached by taking the Laxey road, riding out of Douglas round Onchan Head.

A festival of motorcycling

For the TT, it really is the case that the Island becomes the scene of a fortnight's festival of motorcycling. To emphasize the all-embracing nature of the biking scene during the TT, I have given a brief run-down of the daily activities that took place during the 1989 event.

Saturday 27 May
On the Andreas course, there was short-circuit (by comparison) racing on the South Jurby Road at 13.15. If your taste was for yesteryear, there was a classic practice on the Billown circuit at 19.00-21.30. There was even the Vintage Transport Weekend (27-29), organized by Everyman Holidays.

Sunday 28 May
On Sunday there was something different: the Ramsey Beach Race, South Beach, at 13.30.

Monday 29 May
On the bank-holiday Monday, the week really got under way with practice for the big one, and if you wanted to be really enthusiastic, early-morning practice kicked off at 05.00. The evening session began at 18.15, while in the afternoon, the classics were back practising on the Southern 100 circuit.

Tuesday 30 May
The Classic Race took place between 10.15 and 12.15, after which the modern bikes got on with set-

The Ramsey Sprint is a regular event in the TT programme. There is a huge variety of bikes to be seen, ranging from this blown Triumph to 'run what you brung' machinery

ting themselves up for the TT races for a couple of hours in the evening. For a little light relief there was the Haemorroids rock band at Bush Drew's Pub, Victoria Street, Douglas.

Wednesday 31 May
Classic buffs day, with the Concours d'Elegance and presentation of race trophies at Castletown Square, 14.00-16.00. You could have watched the morning and evening sessions on the mountain circuit, too.

Thursday 1 June
Back on the beach; the Peel Beach Race at 19.00. For 'afters', the *Daily Star/Motorcycle News/Penthouse* TT Carnival at the Palace Lido, Douglas, at 19.00. Events like wet T-shirt contests took place through to 9 June. Velocette Owners' Club members may well have been more interested in meeting at Onchan at 19.30, while all race enthusiasts would have welcomed the big afternoon race practices, usually something of a rehearsal for the big races.

Friday 2 June
If you didn't tumble out of bed at 5 am to watch

A sight for sore eyes – if you own a BSA Gold Star. The BSA Owners' Club Rally is just one of the regular events for one-make clubs
(Ian Kerr)

TT racers through bleary eyes, there was the Vintage Assembly in TT Week at Quarter Bridge Car Park, Douglas, 10.30. Then there was the Supersport Race at 18.15, and afterwards, the TT Riders' Association Lap of Honour at 20.15.

Saturday 3 June
The first of the premier races – the TT Formula 1 – took place at 14.00 over six laps. Then, at 17.00, there was the first Sidecar Race.

Sunday 4 June (Mad Sunday)
Sunday is a real fun day with the chance to ride over

the mountain, traffic being confined to one-way going, then there was the Jumbo Run, which began at Glen Willow Handicapped Home, Douglas. The Velocette Owners' Club gathering at Niarbyl Bay café was scheduled for 10.30; the Ducati Owners' Club (GB) met at Glen Maye, 11.00-14.00; there was the British Bike Rally at Mooragh Park, Ramsey at 11.00; the Vintage Assembly in TT Week at the Rushen Abbey Hotel, Ballassalla, 12.00; Vintage Japanese MCC meeting at the Hawthorne Pub, 12.00; Hesketh Owners' Club gathering, Niarbyl Bay Café, 12.00; Southern Vintage & Tractor Club Vintage Rally, Rushen United Grounds, 13.30; TT

Supercross at West Kimmeragh Sand Quarry, Bride, 14.00; and the Ariel Owners' MCC meeting, at the Swimming Pool, Peel, 14.00. What more could you want?

Monday 5 June
TT Races: 10.30, 125 cc – two laps; 12.00, 750 cc Production Race – four laps; 14.30, Sidecar Race – three laps. There was Grand National Moto Cross, Knock Froy, Santon, 18.00, and a Harris Owners' Club evening at the Glen Helen Hotel, 19.00.

Tuesday 6 June
Another full day of events:
Ramsey Sprint, Mooragh Estate, Ramsey, 10.00
Suzuki Owners' Club Rally, Waterfall Café, Glen Maye, 10.00
Custom Bike Competition, Mooragh Park, Ramsey, 11.00
BSA Owners' Club meeting, Ramsey, 11.00
Honda Owners' Club Rally, Laxey Promenade, 13.30.

Swiss TT Tours meeting, Niarbyl Bay, 1600
Moto Guzzi Club (GB), Waterfall Hotel, Glen Maye, 18.00
Triumph Owners' Club get-together, Ballacallin Hotel, Dalby, 18.00
AJS/Matchless Owners' Club, Sound Café, Cregneash, Port Erin, 17.00
Autojumble, Scout Hall, Demense Road, Douglas, 19.00
Royal Marine Free-fall Parachute Display Team, Port Erin Beach, 19.00
MV Agusta Owners meeting, Tynwald Hill, St Johns, 19.00
BMW International Assembly, Glen Helen Hotel, 19.30
Arena Trial, Palace Lido, Douglas, 19.30
TT Riders' Association AGM, Nobles Hospital, Douglas, 20.15

Specials are a feature of many rallies, and this specimen must be one of the more unusual – a V8 Norton!

Where else could you possibly find such a variety of biking events but the Isle of Man during TT fortnight?

Wednesday 7 June
TT Races: 10.30, Junior TT – four laps; 13.00, Production 1300 TT – four laps. The Velocette Owners' Club gathering took place at the Railway Hotel, Douglas, 19.30, while a Kawasaki Classic 'Z' Owners meeting was held at Douglas Promenade, 19.00.

Thursday 8 June
Vintage Assembly in TT Week, TT grandstand, 21.30
Harris Owners' Club Rally, Mooragh Park, Ramsey, 11.00
Rickman Owners' Club TT Rally, Mooragh Estate, Ramsey, 11.00
Ultimate Street Bike Competition, Mooragh Estate, Ramsey, 11.00
TT Week Scarlett Trial, Castletown
TT Supporters' Club of Germany meeting, Niarbyl Café, 18.00

Laverda Owners' Club meeting, Crosby Hotel, Crosby, 19.00
BSA Owners' Club evening, Rushen Abbey Hotel, 20.00
The 59 Club Barbecue, Coach & Horses, Ramsey, 20.00
TT Fireworks Display, Douglas
Derby Runners meeting, Ramsey, 20.00

Friday 9 June
The big race of the week, the Senior TT began at 11.00 and took place over six laps. For something completely different, there was the Lap of Honour by vintage racing cars.

Sunday 11 June
Beach Enduro, Jurby, 11.30

And this was no special year, the programme is typical.

Following all this activity, could anyone anticipate anything less than a very full social scene as the background to an unparalleled motorcycling holiday? Surely not.

2 Preparation: the bike, yourself and the team

Preparing the machine

The most important piece of advice, when competing in the Isle of Man, is if something has worked in all the races in which you have competed so far, leave well alone. Another is not to try something new especially for the Island.

You will have so much to learn that is new, and so much to do anyway, that you will not need any unknown factors to consider. When I take a four-stroke to the Island, if it has worked well on the short circuits, I don't change anything, with one possible exception – a steering damper.

At the time of writing, my machine was a GSX-R 1100 Suzuki and, on the short circuits, it did not need a steering damper. However, in 1989, the section of the circuit from Sulby to Ramsey was bumpier than before (tree roots do change the contours from year to year) and a damper was certainly an advantage. That even applied to the CBR 600 which took me to a lap at 105 mph (not bad for an old chap, if I do say so myself!). That machine would go from lock to lock at 140 mph on that stretch of the track.

Stated baldly like that, I guess it sounds like sheer bull. However, when travelling over a succession of ripples at places like Glen Duff, the bars shake so violently that, when you first experience it, you wonder whether or not you will be cast up the road after losing the wrestling match.

In those circumstances, a steering damper is more than a comfort. Although it cures nothing, it does make the navigational problem controllable.

Many of the symptoms of violent front-end gyrations can be linked to the damping of the forks, and usually it is the case that the spring rates and damping are just too hard. To argue against what has been said in previous paragraphs, a machine set up with very hard suspension can work well on smooth circuits, but faced with a situation where it will be travelling over bumps at flat-out speeds, hard springing has no chance of absorbing the track's unevenness.

The secret of making the bike work well in the Island is simply to allow the suspension to absorb as many of the bumps and jumps as possible. If you have heavy springs, or perhaps have adjusted the pre-load to a hard setting (effectively making the springs heavier), then the hydraulic damping will have more work to do in controlling the action of the springs.

It is possible to lead yourself down a cul-de-sac here by changing to a heavier fork oil to provide better control of the springs' action. In fact, all you will succeed in doing is to give yourself an even harder ride, as there will not be time for the heavier action to work at the speed at which you will be travelling.

The objective is to use as light an action as you can; light springs, or less pre-load, with a light fork oil to control them. Then the front wheel will have a better chance of staying in contact with the track's surface for a much more comfortable ride. With modern machines having such a wide range of settings, it is all too easy to completely alter a machine's characteristics by making a few changes.

The same principle applies to the rear where, with lots of spare thread available on many units, it is tempting to wind up the springs to stiffen everything. It is far better to leave the spring pre-load in the standard setting and use more rebound damping to provide improved control of the movement.

It is possible for one person to act as both the mechanic and rider of a bike throughout the fortnight – I've done it – but as sure as eggs are eggs, some help will be very welcome. However amateur, someone to act as a 'gofer' for all the odd bits you are sure to need in the paddock, or in the race office, or to fetch petrol for the next practice, will be vital.

The pitstop

Perhaps more obviously, you will certainly need a pit crew to refuel you during the race, and that pitstop can make or break your whole effort. Everybody has to use the same pits and fillers provided, but a disciplined crew can save you many precious seconds, while an undisciplined one can screw it up for you.

It will pay you to ensure that whoever is to do the job gets in some practice. Among the tasks they may perform is to clean your visor for you, and the screen. Some riders have even been known to change helmets while refuelling, fitted with a rip-off visor, of course. It is worth using rip-offs in the Island. If you have ever gone just a mile or two on the first lap and had a great yellow bug splatter right in the centre of your visor, you'll fit one – or even two.

Spilt petrol is always a potential problem when filling under pressure, and it may be that you will need every last drop of petrol that can be squeezed in to put in a couple of non-stop laps, even three. In the heat of a pitstop in the middle of a race, it is so easy to try to save seconds as the fuel bubbles up to the top of the tank. Take time to make sure that the tank is full. I have run out on the last lap through rushing a pitstop.

Conversely, trying to put in too much fuel can be almost as bad. You end up taking the nozzle out of the tank with fuel still flowing down the line, covering the bike and rider. Be particularly careful not to splash it on a visor, since some will 'craze' over and be ruined, as will the race. Make sure you have plenty of rag handy to mop up any surplus.

It is quite likely that the petrol tank that has served you so well on the short circuits will only carry enough fuel for you to be able to complete just two laps non-stop. If you have entered a six-lap race, then obviously that will cost you two stops; you will have to wait twice for the fuel to trickle through the hose, you will have to slow the bike down twice from top speed, and twice accelerate back up to speed.

Exactly how long a pit stop will take you is anyone's guess, but bearing in mind the need to lose and regain speed, and anything up to 30 seconds standing in the pit, there is probably a minute to be saved if you equip your machine with a tank of sufficient capacity for three laps.

Should you modify the underside of the tank to

You will need a pit crew, who can be vital to your success; they can make or break your race. Here, the author receives a fill-up in the 1986 750 Production race

increase its capacity, do remove it after a practice lap to make sure that it is not rubbing anywhere that could cause trouble. It might be touching a frame tube which could result in it wearing through.

Preparing yourself

I usually make my fastest lap of a race towards the end, which naturally means that I'm bearing up well under the physical strain. This is a fact that you might not otherwise have considered, unless you have tried endurance racing. You can find yourself slowing down as the sheer strain of wrestling the bike around the course for a couple of hours takes its toll.

All the usual ways of getting fit for the occasion are useful, of course, but it will pay you to devote extra attention to your arms and shoulders, as they will bear the brunt of the strain. Riders complain most of pains in their arms and shoulders, often finding aches they have never experienced before.

On a cautionary note; you can go out for early-morning practice and get up at, say, 4.40 to do so. You can return to the paddock afterwards, meet all your friends for a cuppa, then go back to the 'lodge' and kill an hour before breakfast. You'll probably spend the rest of the day working on the bike, followed by an evening practice session. It is one hell of a long and busy day.

The real lesson is that you can do this sort of thing perhaps three times in a practice week without thinking about it. Then, when it comes to fitting in the odd round of refreshment with the team, you may well find yourself carried along on an adrenalin high for days, but it is no way to prepare for what may be the most difficult race of your career.

I go straight back to wherever I'm staying after early-morning practice and can be back in the 'Land of Nod' by half past six. I might not get much sleep, but the sheer relaxation is worth a great deal.

You really will benefit from making sure you plan sufficient time 'in the sack'.

Spares

There will be several sources of spares in the Island; big dealers like Fowlers can be found near the paddock with a garage and van packed with all manner of bits, if you need them. Tyre suppliers can usually be found in the paddock, too, certainly at the TT, and even the Manx attracts some trade services. However, if you have anything on your bike that is special, will you need a spare?

Give it a thought. Whatever you may need in the Island, it is bound to be the bit you never had to replace before, and can't get except by phoning the mainland to arrange a panic delivery. It is quite possible to arrange delivery by air, of course – at a price.

3 Costs

This must be the proverbial 64,000 dollar question, simply because the answer depends so much on the style of operation you choose, what machine(s) you run and even the transport adopted.

At 1989 prices, it cost me nearly £300 just to take a car, trailer and two passengers across on the Isle of Man Steam Packet ferry for the TT. That cost broke down into £49 each way for the car, the same for a very small bike trailer, and £88 each for passenger returns, all being peak summer rates.

It would really pay off for two competitors to share a Transit-type van and split the costs. Larger vehicles go over on the commercial ferry, along with the heavy vehicles that serve the Island's commerce, so a party in something like a removal van might be worth investigating.

Having recovered from the shock of booking places on the ferry to reach the hallowed soil, the next job is to fill out the necessary entry forms and, as for everything else at the time of writing, 1989 prices have been quoted.

To enter the Manx Grand Prix cost £75 per race; for the TT, it was £40, as a 'contribution' to insurance costs. By the time I had entered five races at a total cost of £200 plus, paid that ferry fare and for modest lodgings for the fortnight, well I guess I blew a hole in a 'grand'.

It is true that competitors at that TT received basic start money of £350 once qualified for a race, but you do have to live there for a fortnight, and even a modest boarding house costs around £10 per person per night, and I suppose it won't be long before that figure is out of date. At the time, Manx Grand Prix competitors received nothing, although there was talk of a fund being launched by local businesses to help out.

There is one way of cutting the accommodation bill, however, and that is by doing what you might well have done if you were attending a long weekend meeting at any other circuit – camping.

Special arrangements are made at the TT for competitors and crews to camp, in only moderate

The cost of racing in the TT is determined by the same factors that govern any racing: the machine you choose, how you travel and where you choose to stay. You can camp behind the paddock and tow the bike on a trailer, but check the cost of the trailer on the ferry

discomfort. Behind the paddock and grandstand there is a purpose-built site with the necessary facilities which, while not being quite what you might expect to find on the Continent, are quite acceptable if you are really into camping. It will pay you to notify the ACU, when you make your entry, that you would like to reserve a spot.

Now the foregoing are just the obvious costs. Next comes the cost of simply putting petrol in the tank, and that might well include Avgas at £3 per gallon. With the course being nearly 40 miles round . . . well, you work out what it would cost you to practice for a week and do a couple of races; how about a guess at £75?

By now, you should be beginning to get an idea of the financial implications. To them must be added the cost of several sets of tyres, brake pads and oil changes, plus the fact that after the event you will be left with a very tired motorcycle. If it happens to be a 'stroker', you can reckon on a motor rebuild, too – if you are unlucky, you may even have to do this during the event.

Inevitably, unless you are totally devoted to the racing and fettling, or live the life of a complete hermit, you and 'the team' will manage to get in a couple of beers from time to time. Whatever an evening's 'entertainment' may have cost you on the mainland, figure on multiplying it by 14!

Again, the costs of competing in the Island can be great if you have to take the family, stay in a hotel, run a couple of bikes and maybe even have a mechanic on the payroll. On the other hand, a one-bike exercise, fettled by yourself and with a shared van will be considerably cheaper. Add even a modicum of prize money, plus the start money, and you could even end up in pocket.

4 The start

The recently-erected £750,000 grandstand is a tribute to the Island's investment in motorcycle sport because, although it is used throughout the year as the focal point for other events, it was created specifically for the TT and Manx Grand Prix. It has been estimated that the TT alone is worth some £30m annually to the Island's economy by the time all the sums have been done, resulting from around 50,000 visitors making the races their holiday.

The original grandstand was built in 1926 and, for some 60 years, was the personification of an event that was unequalled by, and was quite different from, any other motorcycle race in the world. Apart from extensions to the control tower in the early 1950s, it remained a familiar landmark for decades.

If the grandstand is new, then the giant score- board that faces it is certainly not and is somewhat anachronistic in its method of operation. However, since it has to portray the progress of up to 100 plus riders around nearly 40 miles of track to people in the 60–70 yd-long stands, one wonders how the situation might be improved without an inordinate expenditure on modern technology.

The scoreboard comprises a series of 'clocks', one for each rider, the hands of the 'clock' indicating the rider's position on the course. Each 'clock' is operated by a Boy Scout on the receiving end of telephone messages that plot his particular rider's progress.

Messages are sent from Ballacraine, The Bungalow and Signpost Corner as the riders pass those points, the Scouts rotating the pointers manually from behind the stand as they receive them. In this way, the watching crowd, which usu-

The Leader Board, which shows progress of the first six, while the 'clock' under each number, on the right, records the progress of every rider

ally packs the stands, will know where each rider is.

The Signpost Corner point is indicated by a light on each rider's clock. When this is illuminated, everyone will know that the rider is about a couple of minutes from either making a pitstop – in which case, his pit crew will be galvanized into action to receive him – or rocketing through at top speed on his way to making another breathtaking descent of Bray Hill.

It is usually a he, although very occasionally there have been fast women, the fastest of these being Margaret Lingam, from Germany, who lapped at over 100 mph in practice at her first try in the F1 race in 1984.

The grandstand complex is the nerve centre of the races, incorporating the scrutineering bay, the paddock, the race office, the marshalling area, the competitors' camp site, and the administration and press office. It is something of a bazaar, too, as during race weeks, countless trade stands are set up in the paddock, behind the main building, where you can buy clothing and accessories. Some of the stands are directly related to the competitors' needs, sup-

plying tyres, brakes and just about anything else you care to name.

There is an area set aside for the manufacturers and trade race team transporters where you can see the works' teams busy during practice sessions, changing suspension settings on machines so that the riders can go out for another lap to analyse the performance. It is always worth watching at least one practice session from the paddock area.

As a rider making your début in the Island, whether TT or MGP, expect to spend a couple of hours on the formalities. These include signing on and having your helmet examined like any other meeting, the difference being that you will need to attend a drivers' briefing that will take about half an hour. This cannot be missed because one of the forms that you will receive on signing on will be stamped at the briefing. If you don't present this at scrutineering, you won't get through.

The reason the briefing is so important is that the mountain TT circuit is quite unique in having three streams of traffic passing down the start/finish road, and they could cross over if riders were not aware of the possibilities for incident in so doing. There will be riders setting off from the start line during practice; riders wanting to enter the paddock, having completed their lap(s); and riders going straight through at full throttle for another lap.

Riders approach Bray Hill flat-out, regardless of machine, and that could mean anything up to 160 mph at the start line and accelerating. Others completing a lap will try to get the fastest possible lap time published in the practice results – otherwise they may have trouble qualifying – by not shutting the throttle until having passed the start line. Then they have to turn across the road into the return road to the paddock. Meanwhile, yet others will be starting to accelerate into the stream of traffic. With all this activity, I am sure you will appreciate the necessity for the briefing.

During a race, there is actually greater potential for a mishap because, having refuelled, riders will be accelerating out of the pit lane and back into the

Riders once started in pairs at ten-second intervals, now singly – so it really is not a normal race, more a race against the clock. This event is the 1984 Historic TT race; Rob Claud gets away on his 350 Honda, no. 20, while the author, no. 19, is on his way to fourth place

race; they will be psyched up and thinking only of saving every last split second.

Actually, there are traffic lights at the entrance on to Glencrutchery Road from the pit lane, and in the event of heavy traffic on the road during a race, they will be put at red. They have the same meaning as a red flag displayed during a race, i.e. you stop immediately.

In fact, it is unusual for the lights to be set at red, and unfortunate for any rider delayed in this way. Most of the time, they are set at amber to indicate caution on pulling out into the race. You should keep tight over to the left-hand side of the road before going full blast down Bray Hill's roller-coaster.

5 Start to Greeba Castle

No photograph can really portray the challenge of Bray Hill; it is so much steeper than it looks here. To get the bottom bit right, go left before taking the swoop through the right-hander, which is the bit that matters

Facing the start line for the first time will be daunting, since it will be in the knowledge that it will be the start of something totally outside normal racing experience. It will occur in practice and under the control of a start-line marshal. You may find riders being marshalled on to the Glencrutchery Road in pairs, or single-file from the paddock with practice already in progress. A green light signal comes from the timekeeper's box, the marshal taps you on the shoulder, and you are off.

With the clock running against your number, you are away on your first lap. For the first quarter mile, concentrate on running the motor up through the gears and aiming for the top of Bray Hill, which is the crossroads, St Ninian's. Straight-lining the gentle curve left takes you naturally across the camber of the road, and by then, on all but the very fastest bike, you will be in top gear and approaching maximum speed; with Isle of Man gearing, that will be very quick.

There is potential danger in this situation if practice is already in progress, for while you are getting out on to the road and lined up on the approach, other riders on the course may be approaching you from behind and travelling much faster than you. Without that knowledge, you can create a dangerous situation by pulling out into the path of those faster riders. Keep to the left-hand side of the road until you are going quickly.

Bray Hill

Racing at top speed down a very steep, curving hill, with kerbs on each side of you and stone walls for scenery, is an emotional experience as well as the ultimate test of nerve. To do it justice requires a better writer than I, but it is such a colossal racing experience that it stretches racing nerves to new limits.

Assuming that you are riding a quick bike, that

you have been accelerating for over a mile and are approaching absolute maximum speed on a flying lap, at a point where the road seems about 6 in. wide, it curves to the right and, at the same time, drops out of sight from under the front wheel. Indeed, it is easy to pull a wheelie without trying. With the added complication of crossing the camber, the navigation of any machine can test the rider's tolerance to the limit.

If, at first attempt, that experience does not set alarm bells ringing in your mind, don't try racing the TT course. You will lack the natural caution that will ensure you finish a race. What may be good enough for the short circuits is neither good enough, nor healthy enough, for the Isle of Man.

I can take a Supersport 600 Honda down there flat-out – that's about 145 mph. I could not do it on my 1100 Suzuki. The throttle goes both ways, so should yours until you know your own abilities.

Spectators will have watched the solos leave the start line in pairs at ten-second intervals in practice. For races, riders go singly at ten-second intervals; the chairs go singly every five seconds. This system prevents bunching, an obvious potential hazard when approaching the aforementioned, mind-blowing experience. For the rider making a first attempt on a smaller machine, it is likely to be anything up to half an hour before returning to the paddock. If the practice is early in the morning during September, there is the possibility of groping for miles over the top of Snaefell through thick fog or low cloud in near zero visibility.

Bray Hill was once known as 'Siberia' by older Manx residents, few of whom will be spectators at the barriers closing off the many roads that join it.

Brake by the road junction on the left as you take the final descent to Quarter Bridge

Watchers there will only see the bikes rocketing by at near top speed. Nevertheless, all these vantage points will be packed deep with those enjoying the view.

Cresting the top of the hill, the road drops away so quickly that it may catch you unawares, even after being warned. It will require considerable effort at the bars to move over to the left-hand side of the road to be correctly positioned to take the dip through the bottom, close to the kerb, and as fast as your nerves will let you.

The run on to Quarter Bridge is uneventful, if anything on the TT course can be so described. Braking poses the problem here, as the approach is down through a tunnel of trees, and while the corner is a simple right-hander, there are several potential hazards. Firstly, it could be damp under the trees on a doubtful day; secondly, you may well be starting a race on new tyres (they will certainly be cold); and thirdly, since it will be the start of a race, the tank will be full, which could provide just enough top weight, given the conditions, to cause a problem. Somebody always seems to dump

Quarter Bridge; use all the road and apply caution driving out, remember the tyres will be cold on the first lap and there will be the extra top weight of a full fuel tank

it, anyway. There really is little time to be saved here, so caution is to be recommended.

Quarter Bridge
This is also known as the 'Bridge of the Quarterlands' because it is on the old quarterlands of Ballabrooie or River Bridge Farm. The bridge also spans the River Glass, which contributes the last syllable in Douglas. The River Dhoo provides the first syllable, hence DhooGlass, or Douglas.

The corner itself is simple enough, although when braking hard downhill, it is sometimes difficult to get right over to the left-hand side of the road, the best place from which to peel off. This is due to the adverse camber on the way out, which is where you will find yourself when taking the bend from the middle of the road, as do so many.

The Quarter Bridge Arms is a popular viewing spot for many on a race day, no doubt, due to the 'facilities' available there. A rider having already run into trouble can turn left here and tour back to the pits for a quick cure before going out again for more practice.

Braddan Bridge

It is a straight run on to Braddan Bridge, although the entry point is not immediately apparent. Braking, too, is somewhat deceptive, and invariably somebody will slip here, one of the few places where the course will forgive mistakes. I did it myself back in 1962 when practising for the Senior Manx Grand Prix.

I was on my first lap of the Island, and I had not even ridden round the course before. The mount was a Royal Enfield Meteor Minor twin installed in AJS 7R cycle parts, but a hurried gearbox rebuild in the few hours between arriving in Manxland and facing the starter had prevented even a look round. So, faced with the junction for the first time, I had left braking too late and almost turned right instead of left.

Braddan is a derivative of St Brenainn, and Braddan Bridge takes the road in an S-bend over what is now the TT Access Road, once the old railway line. This is one of those combination bends that abound on the Isle of Man mountain circuit, the essence of which is to get a fast drive out, while rushing in will defeat that objective; it is slow in, fast out here. The good approach is to take the first right-hand portion slowly enough to be able to position the bike hard against the left-hand railings before flipping it over to the right and putting on the power.

Spectating is good here, with seats having been

ABOVE
Braddan Bridge; enter slowly to take position against the railings before going right for a faster drive out

LEFT
The author positions a 750 Kawasaki right against the railings in the 1989 750 Production race
(Island Photographics)

The run into Union Mills; very fast in, brake as you get between the walls, downhill right, then power left out and up the long hill towards Glen Vine

placed on the bank facing the exit, although it will cost you for the privilege. What won't is to cut round the back of the churchyard and watch over the cemetery wall. Moreover, you will get a better view of the bikes taking the left-hander.

Braddan, too, has hidden hazards. I can testify to this, having 'tipped it in' rather too vigorously back in 1974 when riding Bill Smith's F1 Honda four. Changing direction right on the peak of the camber caused a loss of adhesion, but the straw bales (now plastic) were well placed to cushion both errant rider and machine.

Union Mills

Having successfully negotiated Braddan and been photographed with your knee over the kerb, it is a hard drive out now and through two sweeping left-handers that are taken flat on even the quickest machine, although you may have to pick the line

precisely on an F1 bike.

Rocketing out of the last one at full throttle, you will find that the road opens right out to the left, once Snugborough bend. The idea here is to keep the bike on the right-hand side of the road to get the best approach to the entry into Union Mills.

Union Mills got its name from the mill that used to be situated on the left-hand side of the road, just after the bridge. The principal products made there were shirts, which were sold under the 'Union' label, hence Union Mills.

This is a short, but daunting, section, really no more than a right-hand entry into an S-bend, downhill and between some very solid-looking flint walls and kerbs. Nevertheless, it is possible to drive into the entrance, which is just like diving into a funnel after the open spaces preceding it. Although this is the Island's main road, it is scarcely 20 ft wide as you drive in, knocking the gearstick down a couple of notches with the brakes on hard.

It will probably never happen to anyone else, thank goodness, but in 1979 I hammered in on Geoff Brett's Honda 1000 cc RCS Peckett & McNab Formula 1 bike – a real 'fire engine' – and, applying the twin discs very hard, had the left-hand clip-on break off in my hand. Fortunately, I survived to tell the tale, but with an unforgettable memory of scrabbling through one-handed and quite petrified. I continued to tour one-handed right through to Ballacraine before recovering enough sense to turn off the course.

The section itself begins as a fast downhill right-hander between the kerbs, then becomes a double left, blended into one sweep. The object of the exercise is to get the fastest entry into the long uphill climb towards Glen Vine, which means putting the power on hard while still driving through the first part of the left-hander to achieve maximum boost up the hill.

Union Mills does have viewing possibilities, principally those from the grounds of the church hall on the inside of the course. Looking up the hill, you can see the bikes flash into view and bank right/left as they come down towards you – the quick men stand out from the crowd.

It is also possible to get to the road at the very first part of the section, at the top of the rise and next to the post office. However, viewing is somewhat restricted, although there is a pub to hand.

That long climb up out of Union Mills is called

Ballahutchin Hill, after Hutchins Farm, and it seems to go up in a series of steps over which a very fast bike will pick up its front wheel. At the top is a gentle right-hander at Ballagarey, which should be taken flat-out on anything. 'Balla' is the usual appellation for farm, while 'garey' means shrubbery, hence Shrubbery Farm.

A camp site has been established here at race times, in a field just on the outside of the course, and there is some interesting high-speed viewing to be had on the banks of the fields.

Glen Vine

There is a short decline as the road drops towards Glen Vine village. The only feature of Glen Vine is the very fast right-hander, yet another that separates the men from the boys. There are no real markers to help gauge your peel-off point, and you are travelling so fast anyway that it is instinctive to lift your head above the screen. First-timers will probably drop a gear, indeed, it would be wise to do so until you are quite sure how fast it is. Hard, fast men will simply ease the throttle.

This is the only time you should allow any slack in the throttle wire on the run right through from Union Mills to Greeba Castle. It is a couple of miles of top-speed going, and you very soon realise why it is possible to average over 100 mph comparatively easily on a fast machine, in spite of there being some places where you will be using first gear.

Crosby

Following the previous nerve tester, it is a flat-out run down into Crosby village, the feature of which is the curve left at the bottom. There are few greater tests of nerve than racing flat-out through a bend at over 150 mph, knowing that it is possible to do so, yet doing your best to persuade your nerves that this is indeed the case. In fact, you usually require a fortnight to work up to the most gratifying experience of keeping your head right down under the 'bubble' while cornering. This is an experience you will only get on the Isle of Man.

There is really nowhere to spectate on this stretch until the bikes thunder across the crossroads just before the Crosby Hotel, a very good watering hole. On the inside of the course, the pub car park is most popular on a race day. There is even a vintage Manx Norton in a glass case inside the pub, and that really is a sight you must see.

Glen Vine village; an extremely fast right-hander, difficult to judge the optimum approach speed. Try to find a braking point to suit your bike – and nerves

27

The speed down the long drop towards Crosby is largely determined by the speed you achieve through the Glen Vine corner

Crosby village's amazingly fast left-hander – it can be taken at 150 mph if your bike is fast enough, and you are brave enough

The Crosby Hotel is a good place to stop if you happen to strike the sort of trouble on this section that prevents further progress. It was here that I blew up the 350 Triumph I was riding in the 1970 Junior TT and fortuitously coasted into the car park.

As it happened, the Junior was the first race on the card that day and the poor old Triumph Twenty-One, provided by local dealer Hughes, simply would not take yet another lap of the Island. Now it is the custom at most pubs for the spectators to 'host' retiring riders to the odd 'jar' as solace and in thanks for the entertainment. Well, I have to confess that I just about remember being recovered by my pit crew some five or six hours later, 'crashed out' on the grass and not really caring whether they bothered or not. As an aside, that Triumph was rebuilt in 1989 and sold for no less than £2000. Ah well!

Up past the pub, the road climbs quite steeply. In fact, on smaller machines, it could be worth dropping down to fifth for the run up to the Coach and Horses, on the outside of the course, at the crest. On my 1100 Suzuki here, the bike would literally seem to fly for 'miles' as the front wheel aviated. Indeed, all the quick 750s will do the same now.

On a really quick 'tool', it pays to steady the bike by laying as far up on the tank as you can to put weight on to the front wheel and keep it down a little. If you do think that the wheel is coming up too far for your particular nervous system, do what I do and give it a touch of rear brake.

The technique works wonders in the Isle of Man when the bike starts to get out of hand. This is particularly the case when traversing a series of bumps and the bike shakes its head so hard you begin to worry. Indeed, it is my remedy for those situations where the nerves run out. It pulls the front wheel down, and putting the extra weight on to the front wheel usually has the desired effect of getting you out of trouble.

On to Greeba

Now comes the place most people believe to be the fastest section of the course, the run downhill past the Highlander, once a pub, but now a restaurant. In fact, it probably is not the fastest place on the course – I would opt for the run down from the Creg to Brandish. It is a good place to check your machine's gearing, since it is nearly straight and get-

Past the Highlander at top speed and on the approach to Greeba Castle

ting your head right down can produce another 200 revs. Even so, I would prefer to be undergeared here to get the benefit of a better climb up the mountain; you can always sit up to stop it over-revving.

You have now almost completed the fastest part of the course, that is until you know it really well and can go through sections flat-out where a newcomer would roll it off. There are some amazingly fast places for miles, depending on your machine, course knowledge and sheer nerve.

Beyond the Highlander, where spectators will be

The run into Greeba Castle; keep the power on right into the left-hander

confined for the period of the race, is a short, curving, right-hand, uphill stretch to the approach to Greeba Castle. Time is to be made on the approach, for on many machines it is possible to hammer into this section, right up to the top of the rise, then curve hard left and drop a gear to steady the bike to approach the section proper.

6 Greeba to Ballacraine

Greeba Castle is a fast left/right, but with a dip thrown into the middle for good measure. The entry into the section is a key factor in cutting lap times because it can be taken very quickly. Having driven hard uphill from the Highlander, and depending on just how quick your machine is, you may be able to hold on to full throttle right up to the top of the rise preceding the dive downhill.

The approach technique here would seem to be the straightforward one of straight-lining through the left/right, but the hidden hazard is on the exit. As you drive out right, the camber of the road means that the surface falls away. Fortunately, the rugged low wall on the outside is well 'bagged' at the critical point.

It was here, in 1967, that Mike Hailwood and Bill Ivy inflicted considerable damage on Bill's new Ferarri in the early hours of one TT practice day when the car slid down the camber. On a bike, too much throttle on the way out may mean easing back to keep out of trouble, which is just the sort of thing that costs so much time when it is all added up. The real cost will be on the run into the next section, which will be that much slower.

Spectating is not easy through this section, although some manage to watch over the wall on the outside. There is a track from the Archallagan Plantation through to Greeba Bridge, and a scramble along the Greeba River will provide access to several unusual spots where you can get really close to the bikes as they weave right/left through here and on into Appledene.

The rider, having stayed to the right-hand side of the white line on the way out of Greeba Castle and booted it hard along the road, is faced with another section that, at first sight of the narrow,

The entrance to the Greeba Castle 'ess'. Use the drain as a marker, running down the right-hand gutter before peeling off

Fast left/right past Greeba Castle. The second half is uphill, and the throttle should be eased on the exit because of the adverse camber

The run into Appledene; note the bevelled kerb in case you get too close on the way out

RIGHT
Appledene: a fast swerve left/right. Ignore the first right, tuck into the right-hand gutter and peel off left, but avoid the ripples on the apex

twisting road between walls and kerbs, looks like it requires third gear. However, when you know it, you can use fourth or fifth, really going for it.

It starts with yet another S-bend; left, slightly downhill, then immediately right. For as long as I can remember, there have been ripples close to the kerb at the apex of the left, so that it has been worthwhile taking it wide to avoid them and the resulting wobbles that upset the handling just as the bike is heeled over to the right. This part can be taken so fast that the real problem is simply that of wrestling the bike from left to right, as it is with many others.

It is this aspect of literally having to manhandle the bike from side to side that places physical strains upon the rider that will not be experienced in lesser races. Several hard laps can leave the less fit with shoulders that ache severely, slowing lap times in the latter stages of a race through sheer fatigue. My own regime of press-up exercises done during the couple of months prior to an Island race works for me and does make a difference.

Driving hard and slightly downhill, the road really does seem very narrow, and you naturally ride close to the wall on the way out of the preceding S-bend's right-hander. There is just a gentle right before the run down to Greeba Bridge, past the house on the left and marshal's point. The speed can be so fast at this point that I usually notch top gear on a GSX-R 1100, which means that you will be laid over quite a long way. Initially, it is likely to be the impression of sheer speed, created by the closeness of the scenery, that will inspire a laudable caution and cause you to ease the throttle.

Greeba Bridge is a gentle left-hander, approached

at very high speed. If there is a problem here, it is simply that of judging where to brake and where to peel off. In fact, a very simple solution is provided by the Manx Highways Board, who paint black and white chequers on the kerbs approaching many corners.

The pavement only exists at this point on the right-hand side, or inside, of the course, and using the chequers as a marker works for me. In fact, I peel off right at the point where they start, having dropped down a couple of cogs from top. This sets you up nicely to drive out hard.

On the run up through the gears, you pass the Hawthorne Pub, and there are few better places to watch race progress from than a seat on the tables outside with something thirst-quenching at hand. However, it is one of those places where access with a vehicle is only possible when the roads are open. For spectators on foot, the same notes apply as for the banks from Greeba Castle through Appledene.

The rider's next challenge is one of those very high-speed bends that make the Isle of Man what it is. When you have been through the next gentle curve several times, you will realize that it can be taken flat-out on a very fast machine, but beware. All of these types of bends, taken at somewhere near the limit, naturally have just one very narrow and precise line. Gradually increase your speed as you approach them each time; once you have discovered just how fast the bend can be taken, it won't be a problem again.

That corner does not have a name that I can find, but the next left-hander, Ballagarraghyn, was once something of a leap over the bridge spanning a stream that joins the Greeba River. It is almost a mirror-image of the previous bend, but it opens right out as soon as you are on it and it can be virtually disregarded.

Ballacraine

If you have driven hard from Greeba Bridge, the bike will have been travelling for a little while in top gear, so it will be a very high-speed approach to Ballacraine's famous corner. The fame comes simply from the fact that it is the first commentary point and, therefore, is always being mentioned.

Once more, there is a lack of markers from which to judge your approach speed and where to brake. It is one more that has to be judged by eye each time round, and while I use the break in the bank

ABOVE
The apex of Greeba Bridge – the kerb on the way out is bevelled, just in case!

ABOVE RIGHT
The run down to Ballacraine. Use the gap in the bank on the right-hand side as a landmark to judge your braking

RIGHT
This building was once the Ballacraine Hotel. The commentary point on the left-hand side may announce your passing

leading into a field on the right-hand side, it only suits my 1100; on other bikes, you can brake later.

Ballacraine is a good place to retire if you strike the sort of trouble that, while making you a non-runner in racing terms, still leaves you with transport, even at 30 mph.

The name of the game is to turn left and go back to Douglas via Foxdale, which is quite a pleasant ride, especially if you take the very narrow lane past the Archallagon Plantation. Be careful, though, since all the Manx traffic seems to use it to dodge around the outside of the circuit when the roads are closed for racing. Perhaps the best reason to commend this course of action is if you happen to have another machine back in the paddock and practice has only just started. You could easily get in a couple of laps by doing so. Alternatively, the problem could be one that is easily fixed, like a loose fairing or a dud plug.

Ballacraine has other merits, however. The high-speed approach means that it is an ideal place for your mechanic to station himself so that if you do a 'plug chop' here, you can coast off the course, under the ropes, and he can inspect it before you carry on, secure in the knowledge that all is well.

The corner, itself, is one of those that have been improved over the years and now it is taken a gear higher than it used to be. The bank has been pulled back and the crossroads are now wide open.

However, the corner is worth watching at simply because it is one of a series of vantage points that you can string together between here and Glen Helen, riding round the lanes between laps. In this respect, the Island is so different in giving the spectator several views of a rider's technique in a race as you nip up to Ballig, Doran's Bend, Laurel Bank and on to Cronk-y-Voddy crossroads.

7 Ballacraine to Glen Helen

From Ballacraine (or as you might by now guess, Craine's Farm) through to Glen Helen is probably the most difficult section on the course and the last that you will feel really happy about. This is because it is a continuous succession of bends of all types, each blending into the next, with few reference points. It requires real nerve to go through quickly and is even less forgiving than most of the other sections.

Skimming the wall of what was originally the hotel, it is barely 100 yd up the rise to Ballaspur's left-hander, once another of those jumps that have since virtually disappeared. It was so sharp that it limited speed as the bike jumped high into the air, and my old Hughes-Triumph used to tie itself in knots as it crashed to earth in early Manx Grand Prix days.

'Ballaspur' means 'Pointed Rock Farm' but, while looking quite sharp, the bend itself can be taken quite quickly. From the right-hand gutter, it is possible on many machines to take it without rol-

ling off. There are two complications in it, though. Firstly, it is shrouded by trees and can still be damp while the rest of the roads are dry; secondly, the camber drops away sharply on the exit, so applying too much power could lead to a rear-end slide.

The biggest deterrent to a fast run through is simply the whitewashed, solid-looking wall that confronts the eye just as you are committed to the corner. It is probably best to go in fast, but then 'feather' the throttle on the way out. If you happen to have friends at Ballacraine and are riding a bike with an open exhaust, they will hear if you ease off on the way in – many do.

Doran's bend
There is a nice grassy bank on the left on the run down to Doran's from which to spectate. This has two points of access; the lanes from around Tynwald Hill, and the major road from Peel, which meets the course just before the bend – in fact, they are joined by a lane.

At the time of writing, this short stretch was still relatively bumpy, and crossing Ballig Bridge (the Farm of the Hollow Bridge), the road dips down towards Doran's Bend. This is named after Bill Doran who crashed his works AJS there back in 1948. The bridge itself, spanning the River Neb, was yet another jump that has since disappeared. Now it is quite flat, and the run down the hill is simply a case of lining up down the right-hand kerb, easing the throttle and driving round hard left as close to the wall as you can. Brave men, on smaller machines, may not even ease off!

ABOVE LEFT
Accelerating hard out of Ballacraine up to Ballaspur; into the right-hand gutter, but take care if it is damp, and sweep hard left over the hump

ABOVE
Doran's Bend, a very fast left, much faster than it looks

Laurel Bank

A quick passage through Doran's really boosts the succeeding run towards Laurel Bank, a slight rise to a right/left, tightening up on the way in as it dives sharply, but briefly, downhill. Unfortunately, this seems to be one place where there are only marshals to note your progress, although paddling up the Neb might provide an unusual view over the rough flint wall.

Incidentally, Laurel Bank took its name from the laurel bushes that used to grow there in profusion. It is an interesting place to watch from and one that many riders get wrong, simply because they come in too fast and on the wrong line. Access is obtained via the interesting lane from Starvaay, although even a 'full-dress' Gold Wing would not be inconvenienced.

For the rider, on driving out of Doran's, the road dives under the trees again, and it is possible to hold a high gear right up to the top of the rise as it starts to go to the right and downhill. Dropping a gear or two works quite well here, going in to the sharp left on the overrun. At this point, riding almost in the gutter, Laurel Bank comes into view, and while it is no more than a sharp right, it is easy to get it wrong. Conversely, it can be taken safely and quickly when approached correctly.

The trick is not to 'pour on the coals' too hard when coming out of the left-hander. Instead, ease off a little and place the bike over to the left-hand side of the road as you go for Laurel. It may seem a little extreme, but positioning the bike right over on the white line on the outside of the road, or even beyond it, before peeling off will give a better drive out. Furthermore, it will also keep you away from the straw bales that indicate where many a rider has finished up. If you put the power on early, you will get a faster run up towards the garage at the Ninth Milestone.

LEFT
Just before Laurel Bank, a downhill right/left, no name, but quite sharp

ABOVE
From the inside of Laurel Bank; there is road to spare here, and it pays almost to cross the white line before peeling off right

Rocketing up to the Ninth milestone, you need to aim almost into the garage forecourt before going left into Black Dub – perhaps drop a gear

The Ninth

The Ninth is perhaps 400-500 yd up the road, between high banks and curving slightly right/left all the way, although it can be virtually straight-lined. The S-bend, and a couple of others leading to Glen Helen, can be taken extremely quickly by experts; non-experts, however, should not 'go for it' until they know exactly what is coming next and where they should be on the road.

Rocketing up the road, the competitor sees the garage coming into view and the road disappearing over a hump, going left. It appears somewhat daunt-

ABOVE LEFT

View from the garage forecourt. The rider has to commit to this one going very fast and aiming to get close under the left bank in order to go immediately right over what looks like a bridge; much faster than it appears

ABOVE

The approach to Glen Helen is difficult, and the aim is to position the bike on the right-hand side of the road prior to the main left-hander

ing. If you learn the secton well, you will position the bike almost in the gutter by the forecourt before peeling off hard, diving, it seems, between the high banks and dropping down through what the locals call Black Dub, very close to the river.

It is just one of the thrills that the TT course gives me, to commit myself in fourth on an 1100, quite blind as to what is coming next, throwing the bike over hard left as the 'gap' in the banks suddenly appears and the 'straight-line' is made at the critical moment. This is another place where the sheer physical effort is very noticeable; the speed at which you can throw the bike from left to right almost determines the speed through the section. As an aside, clip-ons that I have used on the mainland for a season, and which have never been moved by the most brutal of scrutineers, have been known to move here.

No sooner have you heaved the bike over right to straight-line the Ninth Milestone than it is hard right again. At the speed this can be taken, you achieve an angle of lean that is sufficient to cause things to wear away on the road, if only your boots.

From this, there's just time to straighten up and the road seems to disappear around a left-hander. In fact, it's little of itself, neither is the similar one that follows, but the name of the game is to blend them into one, taken going hard.

Glen Helen

The final run up to Glen Helen and the seemingly never-ending succession of twists takes another left/right as the road rises over something of a hump. This one does require dropping a gear, then it is over right again on the way out and coming into sight of the hotel. The neat and safe way in is to tuck the bike right against the flint wall and drop another gear, if your bike needs it, just here.

Getting the approach right means tucking the bike almost into the hotel car park before peeling off. The bend itself is little more than a sharp left-hander, although the camber of the road does bear watching. The idea of being so far over to the right-hand side before taking it is to enable you to stay tucked in against the wall at the apex. Also you will be able to drive out hard without running over the camber on the way out and having to ease off as the bike slides down it.

The name 'Glen Helen' derives from a Mr Marsden, who moved there in 1850 and named the

Glen Helen is sharp and steeply uphill, while the camber drops away sharply on the exit. Try not to cross too far beyond the white line on the way out

glen after his daughter. There is a large car park in front of the hotel, which is a good spot to watch from. Personally, I prefer to climb up and along the high banks on the way out to get a really good view. Of course, there is plenty of refreshment to be had there, but there really is no way to move from the spot when the roads are closed for racing.

8 Glen Helen to Kirk Michael

Driving away from the Glen Helen Hotel, it is a steep climb up the hill to Sarah's Cottage, one of the more famous places on the TT course and the scene of a special event in racing history. In the miserably-wet Senior of 1965, it was the place where the entire MV team crashed. First, Giacomo Agostini lost it on the way out on the very slippery surface of the adverse camber. Then, on the very next lap, his team-mate, 'Mike the Bike' Hailwood, came round to repeat the incident, finishing up almost at Agostini's feet on the same spot.

There has long been discussion as to how it was possible for Mike to restart the mighty 500 MV up such a steep hill, and the incident has always been shrouded in some mystery. Some would say that it was impossible and that the bike could only have been restarted by running it downhill. Suffice to say that Mike was able to kick the battered MV straight enough to get back to the pits for attention by the mechanics, after which he was still able to win the race.

Many years ago, a woman called Sarah did occupy that particular cottage, while the hill on which it is situated is called Greg Willys Hill. This is a derivative of the original Manx name, Creg Willeys Syl (Rock of Willey Sylvester). However, while the surface of that particular adverse-cambered right-hander is now quite smooth, it is still inclined to be slippery long after the rest of the nearby course has dried out, so it really does bear watching as you 'pile on the coals' on the way out and up.

If you bother to walk up the hill, which is always worthwhile on difficult sections of the course, you will see that there is 2-3 ft of tarmac to spare on the outside of the course at that point, just where you need to use all of the road. While this may sound excessive for a book that attempts to guide the newcomer safely around the course, it is possible to drive right over the white line without sticking your neck out, and to put the power on harder and

LEFT
Steeply up Creg Willys Hill, Sarah's Cottage is on the left. Apply caution on the way out, as it is often slippery under the trees

ABOVE
Sweeping continually left/right up on to Lambfell and ten miles gone

ABOVE RIGHT
Past the Eleventh to take the two very fast rights. Flat through the first, but ease off for the second

earlier on the drive up the hill; but do take a look at it first to convince yourself.

The run up to Lambfell, at the top of the hill, is something like a double S-bend. Once it was a case of standing on the footrests while the bike leapt from bump to bump, now it is very smooth and you can go from lock to lock with the throttle hard on, but you do need to be very careful on a 750-class bike as you straight-line the bends to arrive at Lamb's Mountain, like many of the Manx names, of Scandinavian origin.

Cronk-y-Voddy

Few spectators manage to find their way across the fields to the banks adjoining the road on the way up the hill from the back road to Cronk-y-Voddy, so you can get really close to the action. Like many a spot in the Island, you can find one all to yourself.

'Cronk-y-Voddee' (more correctly) means Hill of the Dog, and it is an undulating run for perhaps a mile past the crossroads, which is not a bad vantage point in that you can 'scoot' along the backroads between here and either Ballacraine or Kirk Michael between laps. Sitting on the banks along here on a sunny day with plenty of 'wedges' can be a good way to pass the day. It is easy to spot the brave at the right-hander at the end of the straight, as they do not even lift their heads above the 'shed', heeling over flat-out in top gear. On the inside at the crossroads is good, too, and there is room to move on around the inside of the course.

Approaching the Eleventh Milestone you do so rocketing downhill, taking the two right-handers as one towards Drinkwater's Bend. This is a very fast left-hander, posing only the problem that you will be in the wrong position on the road to take it to best advantage as a result of taking the preceding right-handers as fast as you possibly can.

Handley's Corner

The objective is to get the best drive out of Drinkwater's Bend along the short straight to Handley's Corner. This means that you will have to ease through the second of the preceding rights, perhaps knocking it back a gear to get the bike over to the right-hand side of the road, followed by a full-throttle drive through the corner.

The next feature of note is Handley's Corner, a left/right between very daunting-looking walls, named after the famous rider Walter Handley. In an age of coloured leathers of every hue, and the general idea that they are of modern origin, it is interesting to note that Walter Handley actually sported *white* leathers in 1930. In 1937 he opined that the TT should go back to its origins and that racing machines should be silenced – a very far-sighted man.

The bend's name is due to the fact that Handley, whose racing career was comparatively accident-free, came unstuck at this point during the 1932 Senior races. He was riding a Rudge at the time, lying in third spot behind the works Nortons, when his attempts to offset the Rudge's performance deficiency came to an end. It is not a place for spectating, even with the marshals in the short drive up to the cottage. There is little chance to see anything of the racing through the hedges at this point, and you will be stuck there for the duration of the event.

You could be forgiven for taking this S-bend as any other; right-hand side of the road, straight-line and exit on the left-hand side. However, this is one more case where due to being in the Isle of Man and the fact that you are riding on public roads, this does not apply. This is mainly because of the

FAR LEFT
Looking down from the Eleventh into Drinkwater's Bend. Two rights flat, but the difficulty lies in taking Drinkwater's left correctly

LEFT
Handley's; don't take the obvious line because of the adverse camber on the way out. Enter just on the right of the white line

ABOVE RIGHT
The author leaving Handley's, close under the high wall to avoid running down the camber; Senior TT 1989 – CBR 600 Honda (*Peter Wileman*)

camber of the road which, on the exit, drops away quite sharply. Therefore, the object of the exercise is to ensure that you get the bike tucked in under the high wall on the way out to avoid running down the camber and, thus, ending up in trouble on the exit.

For those interested in the derivation of local names, Handley's Cottage is actually known as Ballameanagh, or Middle Farm, by long-standing residents. From here on, for half a mile or so, there is a section of typical Manx road; blind, sweeping corners that are very fast indeed – if you know what is round the next one. In fact, it is flat-out now in the run-up to Barregarrow and is little more than

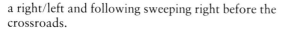

a right/left and following sweeping right before the crossroads.

Barregarrow

There seems to be some confusion over the name of this famous section, which is one of the biggest nerve testers of the entire Isle of Man course. 'Barregarrow' seems to be the popular way of spelling the name, but reference to older sources gives Baaregaroo, which comes from Bayr Garroo, meaning rough road. Like most of the rest of the course, it was once just that. Even as recently as the late 1970s, broken frames were common and suspension units were crucified in a lap or two.

The approach to the crossroads at the top of 'Bi'garrow', as locals sometimes refer to it, is slightly downhill and curving right. Actually, it is extremely fast on precisely the right line, tucking into the bank on the right-hand side on the way in and straight-lining the left curve at the top. Easy to say this, and don't try it until you are familiar

ABOVE LEFT
Approach to Barregarrow crossroads. Tuck into the road joining from the right before almost straight-lining the left-hander through and down the hill

ABOVE
One of the toughest tests of nerves on the course: the run down Barregarrow, accelerating in top gear towards a left-hander at the bottom

with the section, but it has got to be well in excess of 'the ton'. I take it quickly in fourth or rolled back a bit in top.

Bi'garrow is quite a nice spot to view from, although it can get a bit crowded as the seating accommodation on the banks is naturally limited. The best view is from the inside of the course. In fact, it is quite excellent, but from the outside, it is somewhat limited. The section is one of those

where the men who know the way through, and are brave, are so much faster – another case of separating the men from the boys.

Assuming that you have got through in top gear, skimming the kerb on the right-hand side on the way out, you are confronted with several hundred yards going steeply downhill, while the road disappears left around the whitewashed walls of a cottage that sticks out into the road. And they look solid.

What is daunting about this famous section is that you drive steeply downhill, flat-out in top gear and, in effect, you do so aiming at a brick wall. You try to steel yourself not to roll it off too much and to get as close to the kerb on the right as your nerves will allow. The sickening crunch from the suspension at the bottom, as you try to duck under that wall on the way through, bangs your helmet on the tank and bottoms the suspension so hard that it sets the bike wobbling all the way down the road to the Thirteenth Milestone.

One of the most incredible racing sounds that I

The left-hander at the bottom of the hill. The camber accentuates the bend, and the suspension will dip sharply and you will wobble – at very high speed

have ever heard was when I watched Mike Hailwood and Ralph Bryans go through here. Flat-out, it looked, on the six-cylinder 250 Hondas; together, 12 cylinders of screaming four-stroke, revving as only Honda knew how to make them, and 18,000 rpm has been quoted for the 250s.

Viewing from the field on the inside is limited, as now there is a prohibited area right at the bottom, although that was not the case when I watched Hailwood and Bryans. However, there is a rough farm track leading from the top, at the crossroads, to the bottom, and it is possible to get a spot there. I have frequently seen spectators there during races, but do ask the farmer if you can use his field; they are most accommodating if asked.

Looking back up the hill; down the right-hand kerb to straighten out the corner. The author aboard a Dresda Honda in the 1977 F1 race, in which he achieved 13th place

Curving right very fast, now downhill sharply to the Thirteenth's very fast, long left-hander – time to be made, for the brave

Thirteenth Milestone

You are now blasting up towards the Thirteenth Milestone. This is one more really testing section, and one where much time can be made. In fact, it is one of my favourites. There is nowhere for spectators to view, however, as you arrive at the top of the steeply-declining right-hander at a great rate of knots; knowing where to brake and change down is the problem here. The only help is the signboard on the approach that, in common with those at all major corners, gives an idea of what is to come next.

After driving hard downhill and curving right, the following long left is a real joy to drive through, accelerating all the way as hard as intestinal fortitude will let you. The road opens out wide on the inside at what is referred to as Cronk Urleigh, which means Eagle Hill. This is one of the many places where there are only marshals to admire your *élan*, drifting out towards the gutter all the way and notching top on the way out.

There is just enough room between the right and left to treat them as though separate. In fact, when going in on the right-hander, it is as well to keep to the right of the white line, simply because the camber makes the difference, and with lots of power on, it is possible to drift out dangerously wide.

Kirk Michael

Another of the well-known spots, Kirk Michael has access from the outside. In fact, it is as far as you can get by road around the outside from Douglas, unless you have a trials bike and take to the beach, that is. 'Kirk', as I am sure you know, means church, this one being dedicated to St Michael.

Topping the rise out of Cronk Urleigh, the village comes into sight just as though you were approaching the end of the race. Instead, there are still some 24 miles to go! The only real problem for the rider at 'Michael' is finding a good spot at which to judge your braking. Some swear by the telegraph poles on the left-hand side of the road, although they have never worked for me – I have always seemed too busy judging my approach to the village and chang-

ing down a couple for the sharpish right-hander. However, there is a line of them and it should be possible to find one that suits your machine's performance.

Actually, it is a little unnerving, after seeming to have been out in the country for miles and miles, to suddenly rush in between brick walls and houses. It naturally dampens *élan*, but that is good in a way. I say that simply because there is no margin for error through here, and you should always have a safety factor in mind.

It is a popular place for spectating, and you can usually find several riders who have retired at this spot. If you do strike trouble, right from the Eleventh, it is possible to coast down to the village as a good place to stop – if anywhere can be so described. As a rider, and therefore being allowed to be on the course, if you ask the marshals nicely, you will probably find that you can abandon the bike against the stone wall there, cross the road and assuage your grief in the Mitre Hotel.

9 Kirk Michael to Ballaugh

To race through Kirk Michael is one of the unique thrills of the Isle of Man. You pass within little more than 3 ft of the front doors of houses, approaching top speed at that. With a racing exhaust system, the reverberations of your rapid passage bounce off the walls and around the inside of your helmet. Not only does it make your ears ring, but it also leaves an indelible memory.

Beyond the actual corner at the road junction, there are some places from which to watch the riders flash by, but the view is so brief that it seems to be left to the locals, who usually turn out for the actual races. Some stand at their open doors and seem near enough to touch. The road does curve right/left, but the racing line is straight through, although the road surface is pretty bumpy as you drop down away from the houses on the way out.

Before racing through the village, however, there is the approach and peel-off into the Kirk Michael corner itself. As mentioned in the last chapter, one of the complications is that of setting a braking point, but choosing where to peel off is a little easier. As you run down the left-hand gutter, with the brakes hard on, you can spot one of the regular features of the TT course; drain covers that are likely to be on the racing line are painted yellow, and there is one handy here.

That small, brightly-painted cover gives me a good spot to lay it over, one I have used with a great variety of machinery. It gives a safety margin that is just sufficient for comfort, but for me it also means that I can drive through under power, getting a better run out and steadying the bike over what is, at speed, an uneven surface.

ABOVE
Kirk Michael village; the right-hander is quick. A useful peel-off marker is the drain cover in the road. Watch the kerb on the way out

ABOVE RIGHT
Thunder down through Kirk Michael's streets. The sounds will echo round your helmet

Viewers here, seated on the grassy bank by the junction, can spot the knowledgeable, and brave, skim the kerb on the way out – speeds vary considerably. Incidentally, after spectating, a short ride from here down to the beach gives a complete change of atmosphere, with only distant exhaust notes to remind you that bikes are going through at high speed.

Rhencullen

The short stretch through to Rhencullen is one more tester where time can be lost as the throttle hand leaves slack in the wire, rocketing towards the end of the village and the sight of the road curving slightly right, then disappearing left. It is yet another case where complete knowledge and precise positioning on the road will get you through with it on the stop. If you are not in that happy position when you arrive there, ease it off.

A rugged stone wall on the right-hand side of the road, as you leave the village, prevents an ideal run through the left-hander at this point. It is a sweeping, blind corner where a considerable heave at the bars is required. Then there are just a few yards to allow you to set yourself up for the entry to Rhencullen.

Translating 'Rhencullen' from its Celtic origins, you get Holly Ridge, and there is an interesting possibility for spectators on the grassy bank right in the middle of the section, on the outside of the course. Rhencullen can be reached while the races are in progress, by riding right round the outside. Indeed, it is the furthest point you can reach by going round in an anti-clockwise direction. Skirting the course at Ramsey, you can ride round through St Judes and Sandygate, on through The Cronk and then Orrisdale.

Meanwhile, having just wrestled the bike through the left-hander out of Kirk Michael, the rider is confronted by a short rise and a right. This is the time to drop a gear if on a reasonably quick machine; on a classic Triumph, I have experienced the supreme satisfaction of getting through the whole section in top, under the 'bubble', at around 110 mph – great fun.

Cresting the rise, the road seems to disappear sharply right as it opens out wide. Position the bike against the kerb, on the left, before peeling over hard right. The problem here is that the camber drops away quite sharply. The way to get a quick passage through is to get close to the right-hand side of the road to make the best attack on the left coming up, which is the beginning of a flat-out section. As ever, going in fast saves precious seconds.

So Rhencullen is a section that is, simply (?), a fast left/right, preceded by a right. Such a bald description conveys little, but *road racing* specialists will revel in it and make a lot of time here. 'Short-circuiteers', however, travelling at the fastest speeds

Now 15 miles out and at Rhencullen's right. Tuck the bike into the bank to avoid running down the camber. The object is to get over to the right for the next left

The correct position on the road to take the left-hander out of Rhencullen. This is important because of the need to be upright over the hump on the way out

RIGHT
Alpine Cottage can be made a flat-out sweeping right on all but the fastest bikes – when you know it. Much time is to be made by the knowledgeable

and confronted by the solid look of the inevitably white-walled house at this point, will ease off, for a while at least. But that is the way to treat the course while you are learning it.

The left-hand exit from Rhencullen is over a hump in the road that produces another wheelie. That of itself is no problem, but the angle at which you attack the corner can make it one. A wheelie can be something of a problem if you are still laid over to the left, as you might well be. Another difficulty will be the wobble when the front wheel regains contact with the tarmac.

With the bike completely upright, you should have no trouble, of course. However, to achieve this fortunate situation means that you have to travel slower than is really possible. The way to get through fast and safely is to take the right-hander before it in a position that allows you to get the bike upright where it matters – when the front wheel leaves the tarmac, crossing the camber of the road. Until you have worked it out completely, it could pay to go slow in, fast out. You will get faster with practice.

Bishop's Court
Now comes the short run into Bishop's Court, one that always sticks in my mind because you can smell the wild garlic as you fly through here, even with your helmet on and tucked under the screen. Bishop's Court itself is the large building on the left-hand side of the road, which can be seen through the trees. It was once the residence of the Bishops of 'Sodor and Man'.

This is something of a gloomy section, for it passes under big trees. As wide as the road is at this point, as ever, it pays to be in the right place on the road. The next couple of miles make a very fast section for those who know the way round, yet it is somewhat daunting for the newcomer. The road winds along with curves that can almost be seen through. You can straight-line some of them, and just stay under 'the shed' at top speed through others. That is likely to be well in excess of 140 mph on a quick bike.

The first of these nameless sweepers that will test the novice is the left/right that follows the short Bishop's Court straight. Getting into top and tucking right down, aim the bike into the section and sweep through the second half. You will find that a real effort is needed at the bars to go from left

to right. Indeed, travelling at near top speed, you may even find yourself drifting uncomfortably near the outside of the road, by the marshal's point, where the Orrisdale road joins the course.

For this reason, it pays to be positioned accurately so that there is plenty of road to spare, and that means using all the road on the way in, just where, with a wide road, you would not think that it mattered too much. It does, if only for peace of mind. Inevitably, you will find yourself looking through the screen at the marshals at this point, and while it is no great shakes as a place to watch from, you can move from here back around the circuit to Ballaugh and all places towards Ramsey.

Another nameless sweeper follows and can simply be straight-lined. You cannot quite see through this S-bend, nevertheless no slack should creep into the throttle wire, no matter what you are riding. Then on to Alpine Cottage.

Alpine Cottage

On a less-than-rapid bike, this can be swerved through left/right without rolling back. On anything else, it becomes something of a nerve tester, and one more place where time is made by the experts. Its significance is the fact that every mile per hour held through here can be added to the run down to Ballaugh, and that is the way time is really saved in the Isle of Man.

Alpine Cottage, taken really quickly, requires an absolutely precise entry point. Then it is relatively easy, but oh, so fast. It is really just another S-bend, and the name of the game is to set the bike almost in the left-hand gutter before peeling off across the road and trying to get close to the right-hand bank on the way out.

There is real satisfaction to be obtained from getting this one right. You will know when you have taken it to the best of your ability, and I always find myself trying to snatch a glance at the rev-counter when driving out to see if I have managed to get through any quicker. Certainly, it is one more place where expertise shows, but supporters don't have

The famous jump. Another commentary point, and a place for spectacle and high jumps. Straight-line over the hump, 'feathering' the throttle to try to match rear wheel speed to road speed and thus save the transmission

Try to fly level and land on both wheels. The author does it on a 1000 cc RSC Pecket & McNab Honda in the 1984 Senior race

the chance to see, as there are no obvious vantage points.

In fact, there is little chance to watch anywhere between Bishop's Court and Ballaugh, which is just a short stretch along from Alpine Cottage. There is not much to be said about the road, either, apart from the fact that you will surely enjoy it.

Ballaugh

The arrival at Ballaugh seems very sudden, particu-

larly as it is at top speed. After the charge through the previous curve, going right, the short straight to the bridge presents itself. This is a place where much outbraking takes place, and it seems that you are back in civilization, as the crowds are most apparent.

The 30 mph sign which you pass as you enter the village is as good as any place to start thinking about braking. From being on the left-hand side of the road, straight-line brake down into the right-hand gutter, which is where you are best placed to take the famous jump over the bridge.

For the spectator, Ballaugh Bridge is a spectacle not to be missed. It is one place where watching at least once during TT week is a must. There is plenty of access from inside and outside the course, and plenty of refreshment to be had in The Raven pub, which is one of the better ones – it has more character than many others.

Another item of interest at Ballaugh is the small plaque that can be found on a gatepost opposite The Raven. It commemorates the pre-war rider Karl Gall, once a BMW team-mate of TT winner George Mier. Gall crashed there in 1939, and in 1989, on the 50th anniversary of his passing, a ceremony was held in which the Ballaugh Commissioners were given playground toys for the local school.

Every year, there always seems to be somebody trying to set a new altitude record at Ballaugh. I just wonder at the sickening crunch that will subject the suspension to new extremes of stress as the bike hits the tarmac. There are more variations of the

best way to take the jump than you can shake the proverbial stick at. My philosophy is simply that while the rear wheel is off the ground, it is not actually driving. If you have seen Joey Dunlop take Ballaugh, you will know that he jumps hardly at all.

However, the conventional line is from the right-hand gutter in order to be upright when crossing the hump in the centre of the road. The manner in which you accelerate towards it will determine how far you fly and how you land.

If the rear wheel is still driving hard as you reach the hump, the bike will be projected skywards and, having flown, will probably hit the road front wheel first. Cut the throttle just before the rear wheel hits the road and the rear suspension will take a beating as the chain snatches and, if there is a weak link, breaks. The ideal is to try to synchronize the throttle opening/engine speed to the touch-down speed; feather the throttle just enough for a low-level flight, landing straight and on both wheels. That said, after 2000 tries, I still don't get it right every time!

10 Ballaugh to Sulby

This stretch is one of the three fastest parts of the course. Now that the Sulby Straight has been smoothed out, the bike will reach its fastest speed on the flat; from the Creg to Brandish is downhill, as is the stretch past The Highlander. It also contains a section where you can wheelie at 150 mph plus, if your machine has that sort of performance.

For Ballaugh, read 'Balla Lough', meaning Lake Farm Bridge. Having jumped the bridge, there is a quick right/left wriggle as you go out of the village and, taking another gentle right, you rush past a marshals' post where Gwen has stood for many years. Otherwise known as the 'Lady in White' (she usually wears a white anorak), Gwen records the passage of all the riders. This is one of several places around the course where the job is done; imagine

the difficulties in keeping track of all the riders on a course that is nearly 40 miles around.

There is now something like half a mile to work the bike up to speed in top gear as the road disappears around a left-hand curve, which should be taken flat-out, provided your nerves will let you. Immediately after this comes that high-speed wheelie as you leap the hump at Ballacrye Rise. The approved method of attack is to make quite sure that you get the bike perfectly upright as you take it. Any ensuing wobbles and weaves are the result

Advance warning sign for Quarries and a good place for slipstreaming, pulling out just in time to get ahead for the entry to Quarries

viewing places until you reach the Wild Life Park, with the exception of the aforementioned road. At the barrier there, the riders go by at top speed, so you only get a fleeting sight and sound.

Quarry Bends

The Wildlife Park is a good place from which to watch the Quarry Bends action, and there is a lane through the Currahs (marshland) to reach it. This is one of those almost unexpected places where you can find the rev-counter right up the scale in top gear, so the approach is very fast. In fact, this stretch is a good place for overtaking a machine of equal performance, as there is time for slipstreaming after Ballacrye, and you can get alongside for the approach to Quarries.

It is the sight of the road going right out of view, as you run up flat in top, that makes dropping a gear a good idea on a quick bike. Having said that, the Quarry Bends are dramatically fast now that the road has been reconstructed and smoothed out. The section is right/left, right/left, sweeping through and being able to see the line all the way. It is simply the sheer speed, and the fact that you can be laid over a very long way at that speed, that makes you ease on the way through.

There is little to offer by way of advice through this section, simply because, for once, you can see all the way through. Therefore, you will make your own decisions as you go. However, it is one more place where queues seem to form as you catch up with other riders and have to look for a way by. It is only really safe to create the opportunity to pass either on the way in, as mentioned, or just before the big left-hander, going up the inside before your opponent peels off.

Sulby Straight

Now there is only a 'nothing' right-hander before a couple of hundred yards straight and then going left into the long Sulby Straight. Just at the beginning are the Sulby crossroads and the Sulby Hotel, which is on the left-hand side and well worth visiting. Easily reached along the road from Sandygate, its car park is usually packed with bikes, during and long after the races. It has served me many a 'mean' beer.

Disregarding the racing for a moment, if you were to turn right at the crossroads and go up over the mountain, you would be following one of my

The left-hander is the key to the section, so try to pull the bike over to the right without losing speed

of the front wheel not being exactly in a straight line as it regains contact with the tarmac. I have been known to crack the screen with my head here, trying to keep down as low as possible. Try sitting as far forward as you can to keep the front down.

You do see a few spectators here to watch the fun, but they must get there along the field from the Ballavalley road. In fact, there are not too many

Rocketing through Sulby village – a right-hand curve, but flat. The 800 yd sign will remind you to check that there is plenty of front brake

favourite rides. It takes you up to The Bungalow, and going from one to the other is a good way to break the day between races.

On down the Sulby Straight now; Sulby is Scandinavian for Soli's Estate, and this is one place where there is time to relax, if you can do that flat-out on a bike. It is certainly a brilliant place for slipstreaming, but don't make a passing move too early, otherwise your opponent will have the time to do it back to you.

You arrive at Sulby village at phenomenal speed – at normal times, i.e. when there is no racing, you can find a good café on the right-hand side if your tastes are for good plain 'grub'. However, having flashed past it around the gentle right-hand curve, you will suddenly see the bend, the bridge and the 800 yd sign. Now I am not suggesting that you brake 800 yd before a bend, but at the speed you may be travelling on, say, an F1 bike (170-180 mph), it concentrates the mind wonderfully.

It may be that the bike you are riding has fully-floating disc brakes, in which case, given the speed at which you will have been travelling for some time, you could find that the brake pads have been

pushed back from the discs, as they flutter just that little bit from side to side. The effect might be that you will grab the brake lever to find no brakes.

Panic time! Actually, the brakes won't really have failed you; they merely require the lever to be pumped several times to bring the pads back into contact with the discs. However, that moment of panic is natural, so the moral is: don't expect to work out the late-late braking point and get away with it every time; save enough yards just in case you need to use them.

It is worth noting that Sulby Bridge is a place that catches riders out – for whatever reason, they cannot seem to reduce speed sufficiently to have a go at getting round the sharp right-hander that is, in racing terms, 'The Bridge'. There is a rugged wall to confront if you cannot make it, and laying it down really is not a very good idea. However, there is an alternative.

Long experience has led to the provision of an escape route, which is not always apparent at the approaching crash speed. Rushing towards the bridge at excessive speed, you will spot that there are only tapes to confront you if you do go straight on – this is the escape route into a very convenient field.

Now the only trouble with this is that the field is not on the same level as the road you are about to leave – or crash on. In fact, it is something like 3 ft down to the lush grass at this point – it is really quite soft; I know from experience, since during the 1989 Senior practice, the brakes on my GSX-R 1100 wilted under the strain and on I went. The only damage was a broken screen. Hopefully, after using this line of escape, like me, you will be able to enjoy a ride round the outside of the circuit through Ramsey and Laxey to the paddock.

Sulby Bridge is a reasonable spot to watch from, in that you can get close to the action and the bikes slow right down. You might even see the sort of acrobatics that caused one 'fan' of mine to telephone Radio TT that day and request the Nutcracker Suite for me!

There is little to tell about riding round the bend at Sulby. It is a slowish right, taken in the conventional way: outside-apex-outside. The camber does drop away if you go a little wide into the gutter, and the rugged wall is a bit off-putting, while the surface is still bumpy on the way out, up the road towards Ginger Hall.

LEFT
The sign for Sulby's 90-degree right-hander. Depending on your speed, a place to put your brakes on – hard!

ABOVE
200 yd to go, and if you cannot stop, there is a gap into a field just after the arrow

The bend itself is straightforward, although the camber falls away and it is easy to pull a wheelie crossing the camber on the way out

11 Sulby to Ramsey

Sulby Bridge to Glentramman

By 1990, this was one of the few remaining sections of the course still waiting for the modern planing, smoothing and flattening treatment that renders the road more akin to short-circuit surfaces. It is here, and on through to Ramsey, that you will find suspensions sorely tested and where steering dampers can be a help to soothe fraying nerves.

Driving up out of Sulby towards Ginger Hall's medium-sharp left-hander, there is scarcely time to grab a couple of gears before tackling the bend itself. As for the public house, well it is a popular place from which to spectate on a rainy day. If you can get 'pole position' in the lounge window of the hotel, you can watch the riders get wet outside, while getting wet yourself on the inside. It is also possible to get up to the mountain road from here.

Naturally, the approach to the corner is from the gutter on the right, but, as ever, the camber poses the real problem. It is quite sharp here, so caution is needed on the way out as you put on the power. If you are going quickly, you will be using most of the road, and the combination of driving hard and 'falling' down the camber can cause some anxiety. Furthermore, there is an extra hazard when it is wet, or if it has rained recently, since the water hangs

LEFT
The left-hander past the Ginger Hall Hotel; down the gutter and go in late to avoid running down the camber on the way out

ABOVE
Dive downhill into Kerrowmoar. Braking poses the problem here; use the telegraph pole in the right-hand bank as a mark from which to peel off

ABOVE RIGHT
Kerrowmoar is a quickish left/right/left between walls and banks. The exit crosses a sharp camber – be sure to get the bike upright on the way out

about under the trees.

On this corner, like many others in the Island, it pays to pull a higher gear than you might otherwise choose. You won't lose much time and it will have the effect of giving the motor an easier time as the rear wheel hops over the bumps. With a little less power on, there is less chance of getting into trouble. It also helps here to make a conscious effort to peel off that little bit later, as it reduces the chance of drifting into the gutter on the way out.

The following rise away from the hotel, over the surface irregularities, is short, but sufficient to build up enough speed to make the top of the rise another occasion for a wheelie, if you are riding that sort of powerhouse. The road continues right, curving downhill and approaching Kerrowmoar, or what was once known as 'Big Quarterland'.

As you dive into the gloom under the arch of trees and quite steeply downhill, this section looks a little forbidding with its quite tight-looking left- and then right-hand bends bordered by a rough flint wall. Kerrowmoar is one more of those sections where those who really know the road will make yards on those who don't – without sticking their necks out. Course knowledge is, naturally, everything.

Braking downhill and at the optimum point is, perhaps not too surprisingly, the way to get through here quickly. There is little to help judge braking points, but I use the telegraph pole set in the bank on the right-hand side, braking momentarily to set myself up. Then, heeling into the gutter and letting the brakes off, going hard left across the road and getting close to the chequered kerb, put the power back on and drive through hard.

You can see through the first part of the section and are conscious of the kerb on the outside – it looks a couple of feet high, with a background of the inevitable flint wall. It is more than enough to curb the enthusiasm, but here there is time to be made. It lies in driving hard through the right that immediately follows the left, thus getting a quicker run into what is to follow – a very fast section.

The right-hand portion is, or can be, quite quick enough to make you wonder if there is enough adhesion between your rear tyre and the tarmac and whether you should ease the throttle. You should be laid over far enough to provoke this thought if you are making the best use of your machine.

Laid hard over, going right now, it is a left-hand exit from the section as you cross the sharp camber of the road, and at the angle you are forced to do so, it becomes something of a hump. The consequence of this is one more wheelie, but the danger is simply that you may not have the bike pointing in a straight line. When you regain contact with the tarmac, or the front wheel does, you could well be in for a mighty weave and wobble. However, a straight line will avoid this problem.

The Ordnance Survey map shows a track through Close-on-Allen, across the ford through the Sulby River, which may enable you to join the small band of watchers who are privileged to observe the aforementioned wobbles on the way out of this section. They perch up on top of the wall here, which must

be a little appreciated spot to watch from.

Getting a fast exit from Kerrowmoar earns miles per hour down the long stretch towards Glentramman, and that means many seconds saved on the run, which is just over a mile in length. You will be right down behind 'the shed', but it is pretty bumpy and you may welcome that steering damper.

On a quick machine, and until you are quite sure of the road, you may be tempted to raise your head above the screen for a better view at top speed through this section. Actually, the road is not quite straight and you cannot see where it is going, hence the uncertainty and even the temptation to ease off; it is not necessary.

The road does curve left/right and you cannot see through it as you blast into the Glenduff area. In fact, you may not even be able to see clearly through your screen, simply because your head may be bobbing about quite violently as the bike skips over the humps and bumps at top speed.

The slight left/right is just at the point where you arrive at Glenduff (Dark Glen). You may come up behind another competitor here who, naturally, will be straight-lining through. This may well create a problem for the man travelling behind and wishing to overtake, as the actual overtaking speed may be no more than a couple of miles per hour. It is a typical Isle of Man situation and you can get stuck behind for miles, right through to Ramsey. It can get quite frustrating, getting half a wheel alongside then having to drop back.

There is just the odd place to watch from along the way, mostly on the outside of the course. Banks of the fields alongside the course can be reached via the B14 road through Elanbane, but the bikes do flash by at top speed. The one advantage, though, is that of finding a place to yourself, even on a big race day.

Now approaching Glentramman, or Glen Tramman, which means Glen of the Elderberry Tree, you do so curving left at top speed which, the first time you try it, is enough to make your eyes stand out on stalks. What you will do, of course, is roll it back. However, while the road does curve to the left and out of view for a moment, it is quite possible, indeed desirable, to hold on to top speed right into this entry to the section.

Before diving into Glentramman proper, there is just the shortest straight on which to get the bike upright in time to brake and drop a gear as the mar-

Over the slight rise and right-hander, downhill now to tuck into the right-hand bank at the bottom. Then go hard left for the apex of the left

shals' post comes into view. There is a decline in the road now, curving quickly right and dropping down to a sharp left, before which you may want to drop another gear.

It pays to use all the road for this one and position yourself close into the right-hand gutter, holding on a little late before peeling off hard left; taking it that bit late keeps you away from the rugged wall on the way out. For as long as I can remember, the road surface on the apex of the bend has tended to get polished by traffic, and the resulting slippery patch bears watching for, especially when wet.

Churchtown

Driving hard out of Glentramman, you are presented with a fork in the road – you should take the left-hander; the right-hander does have a rope across it on race days to prevent mistakes. Spectators are seldom there, although there must be as good a view as many others on the course, and you could go on down the lane to view at the other end. This merely rejoins the main road and goes through Churchtown.

Through sweeping successions of lefts and rights, it is on to the long, fast right-hander referred to as

Churchtown. It is off-putting through here on sunny days, however, as flashes of bright sunlight momentarily dazzle. There is almost sufficient road width here to be able to straight-line through, but at the time of writing, the bumps hold you back from a full-bore charge.

On a bright day, it can seem like diving in and out of leafy tunnels through this section, and as the curves blend into each other, it is almost impossible to break it down. There are no obvious peel-off points or markers – indeed, there are similarities with the Glen Helen section in the way you constantly change direction through to Milntown Bridge. It is where faster men can really make up time.

Milntown

Churchtown's right-hander is straightforward enough, but it is the key to getting a good run through, in the right position on the road, to enter the Milntown Cottage section. This is a right-hander, but so is Churchtown, and the linking swerve left between the two upsets the combination. Initially, you may find it best to ease the pace on leaving Churchtown to get into the left-hand gutter. From here, you can drive harder through the Cottage and arrive over Milntown Bridge travelling faster, getting the best run into the straight down to Schoolhouse.

Milntown Bridge is another of those humps that have now been tamed. Once, it was a faster version of Ballaugh, and sitting on the wall on the outside of the course, it was some spectacle. Even now, though, it is still a place where the faster bikes aviate

ABOVE LEFT
Drive out of Glentramman and follow the arrow on to the top-speed swervery through to Churchtown's right-hander

LEFT
Coming out of the Churchtown right-hander and into the Milntown Cottage section. Get over to the left-hand side of the road for the best run through as you pass in front of the cottage

RIGHT
Schoolhouse: left-hand, down a couple of gears, then drive through hard. If you get into trouble, there is extra road in front of the bus shelter

a little, and the occasional wobble will get 'Ooh!' from the crowds on race days. To the rider, it still feels like a fair jump, and there just seems time to get it all steady again to quickly swerve right into the straight.

There is little more than half a mile to Ramsey at this point. Just time for a top-gear run down to Schoolhouse Bend, a fast left-hander before Ramsey. You have to cross the noticeable camber, causing the suspension to compress hard on the dip into the kerb. This, and the succeeding drive back up it again, while accelerating hard and laid over, will cause the bike to run wide on the way out. Fortunately, they have widened the road here for the bus pull-in, and while the extra tarmac may serve if you overdo it, the danger lies in not being able to get back on course.

Just a brief burst of speed now, going through the crossroads on the way into Ramsey. There is quite a bump on the right-hand side of the road, so stay middle and left. Next, it is all down to extremely hard braking to first-gear speeds on the approach to Parliament Square. It is here that you may see a marshal showing a white flag bearing a black 'V'. This is to tell you that there is mist, or low cloud, over the mountain, which is not uncommon at Manx Grand Prix time.

Ramsey is the last spot of 'civilization' before tackling the wide open spaces on the mountain. If you have had any misgivings about the motor up to this point, it is time to think seriously about continuing, as the climb to come will search out any weaknesses. There is always the Central Hotel on the left-hand side of the square.

The entry to the square is taken much too fast by just about everyone at some time or other, before they get used to decelerating to walking pace from high speeds. It will seem unbelievably slow, but it will pay off, since running wide into the square will spoil the drive out by accentuating the curve.

It is always worth bearing in mind that you are racing on a public road here. This is a very busy place for road traffic, so slippery patches can develop and, particularly when it is wet, a little more caution is a good idea.

It really is a case of less haste, more speed.

Into Ramsey now and Parliament Square. Better to go in too slow than run wide out into the Square and spoil the run out

12 Ramsey to Guthrie's

There are several places from which to watch the action in Ramsey: all the various streets that run up to the course. One of the better ones, I find, is that just at the start of the incline up May Hill, where riders are peeling off for the corner. Like the rest of the hill, until it receives some radical attention from the Highways Board, the approach is over a pretty uneven surface for racing speeds and, given the need to brake heavily at the time, machines exhibit unscheduled gyrations.

Parliament Square is the haunt of many photographers, and pictures of machines passing Taubman Street, just on the way out, will be seen both in Ramsey shop windows and in Douglas. Ramsey is entirely different in character compared to Douglas, and during race week, the Ramsey Sprint is held along the sea front. It is well worth a visit and usually features a huge variety of machinery, from the professional to the last-minute 'run what you brung' road-rider entry.

The competitor taking the fastest line out of the square will do so from the right-hand gutter, sweeping through the left-hander with the power on hard. Getting into that gutter is the difficult part, simply because it requires extra discipline to slow the bike sufficiently, but it really does pay off, as mentioned in the last chapter.

There is now just about a quarter of a mile straight up, under the pedestrian bridge over the course, and after that burst of speed and quick pass up the gearbox, it is time to go down again. The uphill right-hander that is May Hill almost has a double apex. It is a little difficult in disappearing round the corner, having a steep camber that you

May Hill is very bumpy and the camber is steep. Go in wide, pulling it back across the white line. Use a high gear to save going up and then down again for Cruikshanks

LEFT
Cruikshanks, a very bumpy left-hander; use all the road as long as it is not wet. The camber is steep

ABOVE
Rounding Stella Maris' fast right-hander and up to Ramsey Hairpin. Braking is the real problem, or knowing where to begin to brake; first gear and slip the clutch

can run down on the way out and being sufficiently bumpy to deter the less adventurous. It is a place to spot the experts; newcomers will ride up the centre of the road.

The steep camber continues, as does the climb to Cruikshanks, a left-hander that is just as difficult. Because of the camber, the temptation is to approach it in the centre of the road and not to really attack the bend. Frequently, you will be caught between gears, having to choose between staying in the gear in which you took May Hill, and over-revving, or changing up and not really getting the best out of the motor. You have to balance the extra gearchanges against the total concentration needed in a difficult section. However, in the Island, it always pays if you can pull the higher gear, if only just on the powerband.

The climb continues to the right-hander called Stella Maris, after the name of the house that overlooks it. The high, rugged stone wall on the outside is somewhat off-putting, but this is a fast corner that separates the men from the boys. Overexuberance is the potential danger.

You will now be rocketing in under the leafy ceiling that covers the famous Ramsey Hairpin and makes it quite gloomy. It is a place for correct braking if you are to make a smooth, unhurried, and faster, passage through. There is also quite a crowd here on race days, watching from the area on the outside of the hairpin and parked in the track leading down to the old quarry workings.

This is a popular, although limited, place from which to watch. You will certainly get a first-class view of the machines as they decelerate to 10 mph or so. Techniques seem many and varied, as they go through 180 degrees. You also receive the full benefit of the exhaust notes as bikes go flat-out through the gears, up towards the Waterworks Bends. Photographers really get a chance to fill the frame.

The rider who has taken Stella Maris quickly will be braking on the limit with little in the way of a marker to pinpoint the optimum spot. It looks as though the conventional approach (outside-apex-outside) should serve here. However, the temptation to crack the throttle open, frequently has the bike climbing (metaphorically that is) up the rocky wall on the outside, making it necessary to ease off again.

The better approach to what may seem, at first,

to be no more than a conventional hairpin, is to tighten the line, coming out just over the white line and standing the bike up as soon as possible to put all the power on early. This gives a better run up the hill and also sets you up for the gentle S-bend that curves slightly to the left before Waterworks One.

If you take the hairpin in the usual manner, it has the effect of accentuating the S-bend in the climb up the hill. On a really quick bike, this is something of a swerve, and where dampness lingers under the trees, it is an unnecessary hazard that may cause further easing of the throttle. It is one more case of less haste, more speed.

Waterworks Bends

The Waterworks Bends are two right-handers; the first is sharp, while the second is sharper still, and both are quite blind. The first part can be taken more quickly than you might think, dropping a gear and keeping the speed up while still climbing quite steeply. You will probably need to drop another gear for the second right. It catches riders out on the exit, because it is so tight, the usual trap being the temptation to apply too much power. Some well-known names have slid off here.

Only off-duty steeplejacks are likely to be able to spectate along this section, as there is a steep drop over the wall on the outside; the marshals' post is the only piece of ground on the same level as the road. Further up the hill, I have seen faces peering over the wall, some at the right/left flick (Tower Bends) that follows, on the drive up to the Gooseneck, which name presumably derives from its shape.

The Gooseneck

Tower Bends' right/left flick can be taken very quickly, as long as you are positioned precisely on the road; the danger lies in drifting out towards the wall on the exit. The camber is not obvious, but is enough to make you ease the throttle as you approach the wall. That point passed, you may take the view that the speed of your passage through there was all down to old-fashioned bottle, although medium-powered machines will go cracking through all the way.

There is just a right-hand curve now to place you nicely in the wrong position on the road to take the last bend before the Gooseneck itself. Once again,

it is worthwhile easing off a shade to be able to set yourself up properly for the one where you can make a little time, rather than lose it on the section as a whole.

To the rider covering the twisty 600-700 yd section up to the Gooseneck, it will seem very different if your bike is just 5 mph faster. Hard-chargers, who know where it goes, will make many seconds on the less adventurous. This section is a positive pleasure on a bike with moderate power – sweeping from one side of the road to the other. With, say, 120 bhp on tap, it can be a fight all the way.

The spectator, standing up on the steep banks of the Gooseneck and making judicious use of a stopwatch, will spot the riders who have got it all together. Moreover, the Gooseneck is one of the last places you can get to from the outside of the course to see the riders before they take on the mountain.

This is also a good place to set up a signalling post to keep riders informed of progress. If on the last lap, from here, there is still time for you to make a final effort, if you know it is vital. Races can be won and lost here. As you take the bend, being steeply uphill, you will find yourself looking directly

LEFT
Rounding the Hairpin, sprint up to Waterworks One. Watch for damp patches under the trees

BELOW
Coming up out of the Gooseneck, the author powers away on the Honda CBR 600, good enough for a lap at 105 mph

up at the bank overlooking the corner. It is an ideal place to position a blackboard and signaller, who should be tuned into Manx Radio for the latest information on the race.

You can reach the Gooseneck by road from the narrow lane that runs from the crossroads on the Ramsey-Laxey road. Once there, you can wander up the hill, across the fields, and watch the bikes rocket up towards Guthrie's. It is a good spot on a nice day.

Taking the Gooseneck itself is easy enough; it is a hairpin that you can see round, being a very tight right-hander going steeply uphill. Having said that, it is surprising how many riders do not make a good job of it. The odd few make it look as though they are in a different race, and it is the boost that they achieve in the run up the hill that is very important.

What makes all the difference is getting the braking point just right: hard up against the left-hand bank, laying right over and getting into the apex, as you might expect. Putting the power on early is

ABOVE

At the 26-mile board, there is a slight right-hander on the run to Guthrie's that is a real nerve tester. Easing off here will cost seconds on the climb up the hill

ABOVE RIGHT

The approach to Guthrie's. Taken fast and hard, this first bend can be blended into the succeeding curves to make one radius left into the Guthrie's 'ess'

the essence of this one, simply because there is a steep climb to follow, and every mile per hour you can gain coming out means a higher speed up the hill, naturally. In this particular instance, however, it is even more vital.

The next mile or so is easy enough on a moderately-powered machine: a couple of lefts, a right and then Guthrie's. However, a quick bike will produce a much more interesting ride. Having rounded the Gooseneck, the succeeding left curve will cause little concern, but, by the time you reach

74

Looking up through the left/right kink – left into Guthrie's that should be taken all in one radius, a long left, braking late right into the section

the next one, you can be travelling so fast that real precision is required in positioning the machine on the road to take it. It is one of the many places where, well into a race and getting a little tired, your concentration tends not to be 100 per cent.

The consequences are seldom severe at this point and merely require the throttle to be eased, but, climbing steeply as you are, it will cost miles per hour and precious seconds lost going up the hill. Given that you were able to take those two bends flat-out, the next right-hander can become a real

nerve tester. Once, I was watching the leaders through this no-name bend and, of the works riders, only Hailwood got through without easing off. Again, you can lose a lot of speed so easily.

The real difficulty lies in the fact that the road's camber forces the machine to drift out towards the grass and the marshals in the recess in the bank. This and the bend before are places where 'bottle' pays off, but, in the Isle of Man, 'bottle' should be used with the greatest care – something of a contradiction in terms, I suppose.

Guthrie's Memorial

The final run into Guthrie's Memorial still climbs steeply, but it is just a small part of the total climb up the side of Snaefell's 2000 ft peak. It is around here that the real feel of the Isle of Man's mountain circuit starts to become apparent. There is no sign of life, no sign of a marshal, and only grassy banks and a curving road to see. This is merely a foretaste of things to come and, at first, it is quite foreign to riders used to compact short circuits with groups of people on each corner. The thought of the drop steeply down from the road to the fields on the right-hand side here is a little off-putting.

It is particularly off-putting because, by now, you

Looking down over Guthrie's from the high bank, a good spectating spot and one that personifies the Isle of Man – you can almost see all of the one-line approach

can be travelling extremely quickly, on the right bike. Here, it is possible, indeed desirable, to strike one long curve to the left, through the wriggles that the road makes. Getting it right takes the bike right into the left-hand side of the S-bends that comprise Guthrie's – really one more little bridge over one of the tributaries of the River Sulby.

Walking along the banks up this stretch is really

interesting for the hardened enthusiast. You can pick spots where bikes can be observed through several swerves, the differing riding styles being really quite distinctive. Even on a sunny day, you can find a spot to yourself up here. Taking the time to record riders' numbers and the elapsed time between them that these denote can make the day, allowing you to spot who is really on the pace.

Jimmy Guthrie was one of the great riders of yesteryear. Finding a memorial to him on the TT course suggests that he had an 'unfortunate' here. In fact, he did that in Germany, but he is commemorated here as one of the legendary figures of the TT's past. There is actually room for a few bikes here, near the marshal's post. The view back over Ramsey is one of the great sights around the TT course.

If they ever fill in the ditch funnelling water down to the bridge on the outside of the road, the main hazard will have disappeared from this section. It is quite a deep ditch, and the road surface drops away suddenly to catch out the unwary rider who has taken the right-hand portion too quickly and drifted off the edge of the tarmac. It is one more place where it pays to be slow in, to add power before the apex and then to drive out hard.

13 Guthrie's to the Bungalow

Now for the mountain proper – wide open spaces with sheep for company. It does bear saying that during early morning practice, you may find sheep grazing on the verges. While this is somewhat disconcerting, they are usually so interested in their breakfast as to be quite oblivious to bikes thundering by their hindquarters. However, it pays to be wary.

Having driven hard up the short hill from Guthrie's, there is a sharp-looking left-hander which can be taken very quickly. The speed at which this is taken will make quite a difference to the total lap time, as this is the start of about a mile and a half of uphill going, and nowhere else will the motor work quite so hard.

While you have your head firmly under the screen, listen for the first signs of pre-ignition – pinking – because it will occur here if, indeed, it occurs at all. As a palliative, you may need some Avgas, or to retard the ignition by a degree or so. More likely, however, is that a compression ratio that was okay on the mainland, where full throttle was only used momentarily by comparison, may be too high. You will certainly find several machines retired along this stretch with blown motors.

The Mountain Mile

There are just 50 yd to cover before the last bend, a 'nothing' right-hander over yet another bridge, then it is on to the Mountain Mile. Slight as the bend is, novices do ease it here for the first few tries, a point to watch if you happen to be trying to get a tow up the long drag from a fast machine with a novice rider. Incidentally, it may still be possible to get from the inside of the track to the outside here, by scrambling through the drain that takes the stream under the road.

If you ever doubted the real value of tucking right away behind the streamlining, here is the place to prove a point, especially on moderately-powered machines. On a classic Triumph Daytona, it will cost a couple of hundred revs just to let elbows stick out. A 600 Honda CBR can gain 5 mph by changing an 'untidy' riding position to one in which the helmet rattles on the tank and even toes are tucked in as close as possible.

The Mountain Mile is anything but straight, and it is certainly not flat. It is a long, continuous, gradual climb all the way. You would think that it should not cause problems, but it does, and they are due to the almost imperceptible (at normal

LEFT
Up out of the Gooseneck and on to the mountain; that right-hand kink just past the 27 mile marker can be a tester on a quick machine, but must be taken flat for a good entry on to the Mountain Mile

ABOVE
The Mountain Mile is not actually straight – here a typical kink at 28 miles that will look like a corner in the fog

ABOVE RIGHT
At the end of the blast up the Mountain Mile and the right-hander at the end, this is the view of the approach to the Mountain Box. Hard in, brake late to take the double-apex left-hander fast, and all in one sweep

speeds) curves in the road. They are virtually unnoticeable because they are merely a yard or so long, formed as the road follows the hillside. Naturally, on a racing machine, you straight-line your way through. The problems occur for those with faster machines who may be trying to overtake.

Big machines will pull top gear up this long rise and be travelling at speeds approaching their maximum. Slower machines, with their riders tucked right away and urging every last mph, often do not hold a consistent line, particularly if there is a high wind. So there are lessons here for all sorts of riders and machines.

Slower riders, staying to one side of the white line, will give faster riders an easier time – but they might also reduce the chance of two machines going for the same piece of road. Being overtaken, a rider is tempted to pull into the slipstream of the faster

bike to take advantage of a tow; that is okay, unless somebody else is already trying to do the same thing. So the Mountain Mile may seem like the chance to relax; perhaps you can a fraction, physically, but not mentally, for even if there is nobody in front now, there may be at any minute.

About a mile up the mountain road, there is one more white-painted bridge, where it is time to set yourself up for the right-hand curve that precedes the Mountain Box – East Mountain Gate on all the maps. This is no problem at all on many machines, but if your bike is capable of doing 140-150 mph up the hill, and many are, this one can be something of a tester. Taken flat-out in top, after a couple of tries that is, it presents the rider with a road that does a disappearing act to the left and a daunting view through the stranded-wire fence at the side of the road, over and down the mountainside.

You are now more than three-quarters of the way around a lap, and if it is the third or fourth lap, you may well not be quite sure whether it is the fourth or even fifth; you will be beginning to worry

ABOVE
Through a very fast right-hander, now the Black Hut's fast left; drop a gear and go hard for the Verandah

RIGHT
Into the Verandah; four right-hand bends like the signpost says. Get it right and you take them all in one shot – one of the real thrills of the TT course

about the pitstop and be 99 per cent sure you know exactly which lap you are on. It is the 1 per cent that causes the worry. It really is possible not to be absolutely sure. Some riders have been known to stick bits of tape on the inside of the fairing and tear them off after each lap. If you do this, leave an end free so that you can pull it off, but double it over so that it does not stick to your glove.

Snaefell

Now you really are up on Snow Mountain, which is what Snaefell means. East Mountain Gate was

here, also little in the way of road to spare if you are going quickly.

There will have been little opportunity for the spectator over the last couple of desolate miles, but someone equipped with a serious green-laner can combine watching with rough-country pleasure by exploring the tracks up from Ginger Hall and Churchtown to 'the Gate', together with miles of unobstructed grassy banks.

Continuing the climb up the mountain from East Mountain Gate, the road just eases left and right, but by no more than its width. This is no problem in the normal course of events, but when it is foggy up here, the slightest hint of a curve in the white line that you are following can cause near panic and a parking spot on the grassy bank.

The section around here, and on through to Windy Corner, can be the place for drifting low cloud. This is not so bad, but Manx Grand Prix riders can encounter real fog, right from Guthrie's to the stretch coming down to Creg-ny-Baa. TT riders seem not to be sent out in quite such bad conditions. A close study of the white lining, while the road is clear, can be a great help – the space between the lines is reduced on the approach to a bend.

There is another of those no-name bends next, right-hand and looking sharper than it is. Actually, it can be taken very quickly indeed – flat-out on most bikes. The Stonebreakers Hut comes into view as you rocket uphill. However, if you ride down the other way when the roads are open, the road also looks uphill! An interesting optical illusion.

The more popularly known name for this fast left-hander is the Black Hut, and it is one more place to lose time if you slacken the 'wire' too much. It is probably better to drop a gear and pile it on. The road still climbs, going up to The Verandah, and there is no doubting this one. A large sign says, 'Four Bends', and they blend one into the next all the way around this long right-hander.

On a really quick bike, it is possible to take all four Verandah Bends in one swoop. Start from the outside of the white line on the first part, be on the white line at the second, inside at the third and practically tucking in under the bank on the inside on the way out at full throttle. Getting this one just right leaves you with a feeling of satisfaction all the way down the road to the Les Graham Memorial, or Bungalow Bridge as it is sometimes called. Les Graham contributed much to the development pro-

the name of the gate across the road at this point when it was little more than a rough track. The first rider up the hill had the task of opening it for the others to follow during practice. The bend itself is a double-apex, very fast left-hander that sets you up for the continuing climb towards the Black Hut.

Late braking and the correct peel-off point are particularly critical here. There is the usual signpost on the approach to the corner to let you know which way it goes, and that should allow you to set yourself up on the brakes, depending on your speed, bike, and quotient of bravery. It is taken by peeling off late and trying to apex the second part of the bend. There are precious few useful landmarks

Bungalow Bridge is a very fast left-hander. Spot the drain in the right-hand gutter on the way in as a peel-off point

gramme that made the MVs such a success in the early 1950s.

Bungalow Bridge is a very fast left-hander that, for a change, you can see right through, so it is relatively easy. There is the almost customary adverse camber on the way out, but on the way in, there is little to set yourself up by. However, if you have an eagle eye, you may be able to spot my own marker, a drain in the right-hand gutter.

On a sunny day, you will see some spectators around the banks. You can ramble around here from the Bungalow and on down to the Black Hut if you really feel energetic. There are some fine pictures to be taken along here, using the background scenery out towards Laxey to give a real mountainous, Isle of Man feel to the picture.

The Bungalow

The last piece of road before the rider tackles the Bungalow section is almost another Verandah in miniature. The three rights that precede the Bungalow blend into one long sweep, and it is essential to end up in the right place for what is to come. The aim is to finish on the right-hand side of the road. Spotting exactly where to haul the bike hard across the road is the difficult bit, although there is a landmark on the road itself. The central white line becomes a solid line at about the right point, and whether you choose to peel off before or after, it is something from which to gauge your approach.

The Bungalow is a popular viewing spot for many. It can be reached from the inside of the course from Ginger Hall and the Sulby crossroads, one of

my favourite rides. From the outside, non-motorized spectators can use the electric railway from Laxey, after taking the tram from Douglas. That ride will give you views that are not to be missed.

An alternative for the energetic or green-laner is to use the track that passes the great waterwheel, 'The Lady Isabella', in Laxey, and continues up through Agneash to the old mine workings, then go across the field right up to the fence. If you are on the inside of the course, refreshments are to be had at Murray's Motor Museum. The hundreds of historic bikes are well worth a view, too.

The key to getting through the Bungalow quickly – and safely – is to take a tight line that avoids running out wide as you cross the railway lines. It is achieved by starting from the right-hand gutter and pulling hard into the grassy apex early. This will allow you to put the power on early and keep the

This view through the Bungalow section is deceptive in that it drops in quite steeply and can catch out the unwary as they cross the tram lines

bike completely upright as you cross the rails. This is particularly important if it is wet, as they will be quite slippery. Since you will be travelling downhill for this first part, it pays to pull a high gear, which avoids the need to change half-way through, just as the bike bucks over the lines.

Finally, you are faced with a road that climbs up Hailwood Rise to the Heights of that ilk and then Brandywell, the highest part of the course. From there, it is all (well, mostly) downhill going, and it is possible to get back to the start by coasting and pushing, if you really must. If it means finishing in a race rather than retiring on the last lap, many do just that.

14 Bungalow to the finish

Having put the power on early, the rider should get a fast run up the rise towards Brandywell with its deceptively fast left-hander. After climbing for perhaps half a mile from the Bungalow, first there is a gentle right that completely obscures the point at which to peel off for the real corner. It is one where holding on late, before laying it over hard, pays off, as the apex seems to be somewhat further round the corner than it first appears.

This can be a good spot from which to watch; there is an access road up the inside of the course from Injebreck and the top of Barregarrow. It is one of those bends where the experts will be much faster than the rest. At this point, the competitor has *only* about six miles to go to complete the lap – a distance equivalent to a complete short-circuit club race. An unusual viewing spot is at the point where the machines come out of this one, watching through the fence here – the bikes appear head-on and pass very closely, providing an opportunity for excellent pictures.

Sweeping quickly round that left-hander, there is just a gentle right before tackling one of the particular features of the mountain; the Thirty-Second Milestone. You get a real impression of racing down the mountain now, and the lack of a bank on the outside reminds you of the drop down the side of the mountain, inducing a certain slackness in the throttle. It is at this point, however, that you need to hang on towards the outside to achieve, as usual, a late peel-off.

The Thirty-Second consists of three left-handers, which can just about be blended into one – at least, the top men will do so; there is time to be made here. Getting this one right means staying out wide for the first part, passing very close to the apex of

RIGHT
Brandywell itself is a straightforward enough, fast left-hander, but correct positioning on the way in is essential; go in very late

ABOVE FAR RIGHT
The second of the three lefts is the key; the apex is just under the marshalling point that you can see under the shelter just visible in the picture

FAR RIGHT
The downhill run to Windy Corner, a good place for overtaking on the brakes

the second, and running out wide on the exit. The run down to Windy Corner will be so much quicker when you get this one just right.

Windy Corner

This corner is aptly named, for there always seems to be a strong wind funnelling up the valley, and on a really blustery day, it can pose a danger. On occasion, the wind can be quite strong enough to blow the bike off course, even to cause a crash. It is usually most apparent just as the machine is heeled right over, when it can get underneath, giving the impression that it is going to blow the front wheel right away.

Windy is quite a popular place from which to view because there is access from the outside, up the hill from Glen Roy. This is a rough track, but several intrepid car drivers manage to trek up here on a race day. It is easy enough on a bike, however, and once there you can walk along the banks to the Thirty-Second, or along to the Thirty-Third.

It is a fair rush down to Windy, and you could even notch top on a quick bike, just to make the point. The section is a good test of brakes and the place where overtaking moves are made. The bend is straightforward where short-circuit men can

shine, being about 80 degrees right. Then comes some flat-out swervery, on any bike, on the run down towards the Thirty-Third Milestone.

This stretch is another place for tucking tightly away to gain that last mile per hour and slipstreaming other bikes for that overtaking move to get a clear run through towards what is, quite simply, a brave man's corner. Its double-apex left-hander should be taken as one and, as usual, getting the entry right is the essence of success. There is a gentle right curve before it which, on a Superbike, can be quite a struggle; it is no trouble on a medium-powered bike. The effect, though, is to force the bike into the wrong position to enter the part that really matters, so you need to make it a little tighter than it really is.

From the right-hand side of the road, peel off from the first of the yellow fence posts here, a very useful marker when it is foggy. While you will build up to racing speed after several tries, it really is a case of charging in, running wide initially, but the right line will bring you into position, tucking in almost under the bank on the way out. Here, the road suddenly opens right out, and you will wonder why you eased off.

It is possible to spectate here if you fancy a hike

ABOVE FAR LEFT
Windy Corner, a scratchy right-hander, but the wind can pose a problem by getting under the front wheel – and there is always some wind!

FAR LEFT
Begin to tuck the bike in hard right against the fence. Peel off by the start of the yellow fence posts – double-apex left and very fast

LEFT
From Keppel down to Kate's Cottage, just visible on the skyline. Downhill and very fast left, caution needed on very fast bikes

on a nice day, up from the Creg. Standing right on top of the high bank provides a fine view, and you can see bikes all the way down from the Thirty-Second, through Windy and down to Keppel. It is one of the few places where you can see the bikes over a stretch of a mile or two.

Keppel Gate

After a couple of hundred yards, it is a heavy braking job as you enter the easy right-hander before Keppel Gate proper. Although called Keppel Gate today, it was known as Hero's Gate in years gone by. It is a slight right and a hard left. Inevitably, you will find yourself braking and changing down, while laid over, as you scrabble right into the gutter before laying hard down to go left.

You cannot fail to notice the sea of faces watching your progress on a race day, both inside and outside the course. On the inside, there is a convenient car park in which you can watch from the bank, but you will be there until the roads are re-opened. On the outside of the course, many walk up from the Creg, quite an exercise, but it provides the opportunity to visit many spots on foot. It is another good spot for photographers.

Driving out hard, there is a short blast down to Kate's Cottage. There was a Kate once, but before her, the cottage was the home of a Mr Tate, a shepherd who was in charge of the hills around here, many years ago. This is yet another place to spot the brave men, who will bore through here, really going for it. The timid types will betray themselves by their exhaust notes as they ease the throttle. Road engineering took the problems out of this one during the winter of 1988.

Creg-ny-Baa

Having rocketed out of Kate's Cottage, fast men may actually pull wheelies while driving hard downhill towards the Creg. It is really steep down here, and braking is the problem. Fortunately, there is a slip road if you cannot stop, going slightly left around behind the hotel and usually giving enough space to stop, even if the pads have become glazed.

'Creg-ny-Baa' is how it is spelt, but Manx purists would pronounce it 'Kreg na Bay'. The Keppel Hotel on this corner is an excellent place from which to watch, as all the usual comforts are to be had. Sitting up on the balcony in the sunshine, with the Manx Radio commentary for information, is a

LEFT
The view from Kate's and down to the Creg

ABOVE
Looking back up to Kate's, shows just how steep the drop really is – the author on a Kawasaki

ABOVE RIGHT
View over the Creg. Let it all hang out on this short-circuit-style, quite fast right, but use caution as it is often damp right on the apex

pleasant way to spend an afternoon. The slip road runs right back to the Douglas-Laxey road, so you can move to other spots, and there is ample car parking space in the nearby field.

As mentioned, stopping is the real problem at this one because there is so little from which to judge a braking point. Travelling very fast downhill, you will find it to be one of the real testers. It is something of a short-circuit corner in nature, but may have a hidden hazard. On all but the sunniest days, there always seems to be the suspicion of a wet

patch on the apex. It is probably due to an underground stream, but the patch is always on the racing line, and it catches somebody out almost every year.

The run down to Brandish is probably the fastest part of the course, completely smooth and with just a gentle curve right before the final descent to the sharp left-hander itself. At around 160 mph, though, it looks about 6 in. wide from behind the screen. The corner takes its name from another of the stars of days gone by: Walter Brandish, who tumbled there in 1923. Like many others, he may have misjudged the braking point – watching the rev-counter needle climbing to new heights can contribute to that. As an aid to peeling off, there is a break in the bank on the right-hand side, an entry into the field.

Hillberry

The road continues to drop down to Hillberry, being completely straight, so it is back up to top gear. There are just a couple of miles to the finish. Hillberry is the English form of the original Manx name, Cronk y Berry, Berry being a legendary Manx witch. There is a rough grandstand erected on the

ABOVE

Brandish itself is a fast left-hander; a useful peel-off point is the break in the bank on the inside of the course, just by no. 34 – the author leads
(Island Photographics)

RIGHT

Another flat-out run, this time down to Hillberry, a very fast right-hander. Hard against the low wall, drop a gear and go in hard

entry to this one. It is a fine place to watch the bikes sweep through at high speed. It is also possible to get there from the narrow lane through Onchan.

That right-hand swoop through Hillberry will gain, or lose, you time on the quite steep climb up to Cronk ny Mona, or Hill of the Turf. It is the last hill before the finish, and if 'the donkey has died', you can push up here to make it to the pits. The course swerves left now, although the minor road that goes straight on was part of the course in earlier days. This point does attract a few viewers on race days. Indeed, some manage to gain a vantage point on the long wall right around this section.

Signpost Corner

The road around Cronk ny Mona's long left-hander is not a true radius, but it can be made into one and taken very quickly indeed. Taking it from hard against the right-hand kerb, achieving that one-line curve requires staying out over to the right of the white line for the first half and gradually pulling the bike across towards the exit. Then it is downhill to Signpost Corner, where you will need to be on the left-hand side of the road.

Signpost is straightforward enough, a scratchy right where short-circuit exponents will hang it all out and go for it. There is a slip road if you misjudge braking, and the road is downhill here, but the temptation is to try to get round with the brakes on, and many get away with riding up the high grassy bank on the way out. This is a good place from which to watch; seated up on the bank, along the road to Bedstead, you get so close to the bikes – a unique aspect of the races in the Island.

From Signpost, your passage through will be reported to the Boy Scouts who operate the huge scoreboard in front of the grandstand. A light will be switched on over your number to indicate your passing and to prepare your pits for your arrival in a couple of minutes.

Bedstead's fast left holds no terrors now, having been largely reconstructed, but it does have a character of its own and there is a sort of 'wall of death' feeling about it. Riding hard down the right-hand kerb on the way in, the trick with this one is to hang

on late and really attack the bend short-circuit style, diving into the apex while riding down the camber. This gives the impression of looking up at the road, so far are you laid over. The really good part is the exit, where the kerb has been omitted and, *in extremis*, you can ride up the pavement to get out of trouble.

The Finish

Racing downhill still, you come to The Nook, a right-hand, sharpish corner that takes its name from the house opposite, which is the home of the Lieutenant-Governor. It is one more test of the brakes and, by now, they may be becoming really tired after crash-braking at the Creg, Brandish, Signpost and Bedstead. You dive in under trees at this quite sharp right-hander, and the road seems narrower as a consquence.

This starts the swerving run down to Governor's Bridge, a sharp drop to the Hairpin and the sharpest corner on the TT circuit. The road seems to narrow further and suddenly you are confronted with the need to bang the brakes on hard to reduce the pace to what, at first, seems a quite silly speed, say 10 mph. Fortunately, there is a run-off area, which many use, but if you are pushing in, you will need to go right down into the Dip; taking the main road around the outside will disqualify you.

So slow do you need to go to take the right-hand, first portion of this section that on a racing bike, you will probably declutch; a production bike will

ABOVE LEFT

The entry to Cronk-ny-Mona; a very long left and very fast when you can get it all in one long curve. The road going to the right was once part of the course

LEFT

Signpost Corner; braking is often the problem, as the approach is downhill. The arrow in the picture is the second one and a useful peel-off point. Short-circuit style and a favourite place for photographers. Put your best knee forward!

RIGHT

Hard out of Bedstead and down to the start of the Governor's Bridge section. It has a bumpy, downhill approach where the experts make a lot of time

RIGHT
Looking through the first right-hander and down to the left leading to Governor's One; braking is the problem here, but there is road to spare

ABOVE FAR RIGHT
The last corner is to come now: Governor's Hairpin, a very slow left-hander. Get right against the wall on the way in
(*Island Photographics*)

FAR RIGHT
Coming out of the Dip. Mind the camber and get close to the right-hand kerb, like Roger Marshall on the works Skoal Bandit Suzuki

trickle round in first on the overrun. Down into the Dip now on what was once the main Douglas–Onchan road. It is bordered by trees and frequently slippery, and so slow that it is a mistake to try to rush it. Overtaking a slower rider can be tempting, but it can provoke contact and spills, so narrow is the racing line.

Achieving the best run up to the Glencrutchery Road requires tucking in close under the wall to straight-line, as far as is possible, the drive up the short rise out. Nevertheless, it will be a curve and the bike will cross the camber. With the temptation to 'go for broke' for the fastest run to the flag, this can pose a problem. However, now you are back on 'The Road of Harper's Glen', once the name of Glencrutchery Road, and that is a lap.

15 The track – a history since 1962

The circuit has changed over the years almost out of all recognition in places. Once upon a time, riders were lifted from their machines at the end of a race, completely exhausted. In the main, this was due to the battering that they took from the uneven road surfaces and rudimentary suspension of their machines.

Even as recently as 1986, the surface of the Sulby Straight was so rough that it prevented some riders from holding the throttle wide open, despite the fact that it is straight for something like 1.5 miles. In fact, I have known a twin-shock bike, at around 150 mph, to leap around so much that it really was difficult to see properly. Also there was the real fear that the oscillations at the bars would develop into something worse – indeed, for some they did.

Naturally, the changes have made for a much easier ride, and the very character of the course has been changed by so many 'improvements'. At the time of writing (1989), there are precious few sections of the road that really retain their original character, but one that does come to mind is that from Sulby Bridge to Ramsey.

There have been many tries at estimating just how much the changes have contributed towards the amazing lap speeds that are achieved today. Undoubtedly, the virtual rebuilding of Quarry Bends – there is no other description that really fits – has cut many seconds off all riders' lap times. Other minor alterations, like the easing of the bends at Ballacraine and Sulby Bridge, contribute split seconds.

I hold the view that the real stars have gained rather less than the midfield men, like myself. Now we can go faster in places where previously only race winners had the nerve to hold the bike at winning speeds, wobbling and weaving over bumps and jumps so bad that muscles neared the limits of their endurance simply with the effort of fighting the bike through the corners.

These days, the real heroes go through just a *little* quicker because the contour of the bend is *still* there, but the lesser lights are encouraged by the smooth surface to knock seconds off their lap times. Today, one can see short-circuit riders tackling the Island for the first time with knees out, even riding on their knee-scrapers, and not only getting away with it, but putting in good performances, too.

Not so long ago, such riders would have had to change their riding style to make a reasonable job of the TT. Now, this is not necessarily the case, although the smooth 'stay with the bike' style is still the best way to engender the state of mind that contributes to a creditable performance after two weeks of tackling the world's toughest road-racing challenge.

In 1989 I wrote a short review of the changes for *Motorcycle Sport*, looking back over all I could remember since starting to compete there back in 1962 in the Senior Manx Grand Prix. That report is reproduced below.

During race time, any visitor will see, in shops selling race photographs, pictures of Agostini riding the works MV Agusta with the wheel about 3 ft in the air, or even the stars of yesteryear, standing on the footrests of their Manx Nortons and fighting the bikes down Bray Hill.

It was the lumps, bumps and humps that existed at the time in the road surface that caused riders of 125 mph machines to roll it off. Now, even at 145 mph on a CBR Honda 600, I can go through flat-out. This must have saved at least three seconds on the road for most of the midfield, although the stars of every year, no doubt, were of the calibre that would have got through the section flat-out, no matter what they were riding.

Quarter Bridge, while it has changed visibly in possessing a mini-roundabout and silky-smooth surface, nevertheless is *little* faster. There is still an

Werner Haas on a 250 NSU leads down Bray Hill. It does not look too bad, but in those days, the limiting factor was the surface, which was akin to a scrambles track; it certainly tested the rudimentary suspensions

adverse camber on the way out that presents a hazard on new tyres with a full tank. Indeed, it usually catches somebody out each year.

The approach to Union Mills is one that bears no resemblance to yesteryear. Once there was a tricky right-hander called Snugborough, which was smoothed out completely in the mid 1970s and now allows one to bore hard into Union Mills with the throttle wide open until reaching the entry. It must be worth at least a couple of seconds, while the exit from Union – downhill past what were the old woollen mills – having lost most of its bumps, must be worth another half.

Right through to Ballacraine, the bends themselves have changed little in outline, but now the road is truly level and the ride is certainly easier. Where once the stars wrestled their ill-handling bikes through at full speed and the rest wilted, now 'the rest' can narrow the distance between themselves and the 'greats'.

Ballacraine has been affected by the road improvements, the apex having been pulled back as well as smoothed, which allows the use of a higher gear than previously and gives a faster run up to Ballaspur. This may cut another second off lap times.

Ballaspur itself was once a jump approaching Ballaugh standards. In the early 1960s I nearly went over the wall there, simply because of the wobbles inspired by the jump over the hump and the succeeding irregularities that would tie the Triumph's frame in knots. Now it is only a problem on the

fastest bikes, as the bend itself is only medium-fast, using all of the road. The change must give another second.

Essentially, the circuit right through to the Glen Helen Hotel has not changed, and even Sarah's Cottage still catches riders out with its adverse camber and lingering moisture under the trees. However, the following Creg Willys Hill is another section that would hardly be recognized by riders from a decade ago.

The successions of surface irregularities were once almost evil in the way they would throw a bike about, and early production machines with their elastic frames were quite frightening up there. The Highways Board's efforts have dismissed all but the smallest bumps, and the brave will not ease off even the quickest bikes now. It is another situation where the real 'hard' men would have wrestled through, standing on the footrests, while the wimps outside the first dozen would have rolled it back. At least for them, the savings must have been a second or so, just for peace of mind.

Now it is possible, even on an 1100, to enter the Cronk-y-Voddy Straight at full bore, engaging top quite early. When Cronk-y-Voddy was bumpy, it was common for bikes to get completely out of hand, even going up that straight; my own BMW was almost written off there by my co-rider when practising for the 1976 ten-lap Handicap Race. The bike threw him off and tried to move the earthbank at the crossroads, three-quarters of the way up there. It certainly caused a severe pain in the wallet.

ABOVE LEFT
This is how Sulby Bridge looked in 1968 as the author led the 500 Production race. Since then, the apex has been pulled back some way and smoothed right out. It is now a faster bend, but otherwise this part has not changed very much

LEFT
Ginger Hall, as it looked three decades ago. The bend itself is still the same, although the surface is better, and it poses the same problems with the same adverse camber on the exit

ABOVE
Creg-ny-Baa as it was in 1954. The contour of the bend has not changed at all, but because it is so smooth now, everybody 'goes for it' and, inevitably, there are spills

A recent resurfacing of the bend, at the end of the straight, has removed the terrors of the approach to the Eleventh Milestone. In the 1960s, I watched Hailwood take the Honda Six through there, flat on the tank. Pursuers, on Manx Nortons, were dropping down a gear. Until recently, it was

quite unkind at the speeds attainable by present-day bikes. Now you sweep through with the throttle wide open and save another second or so.

There have been no major changes from this point right through to Quarry Bends, where the only phrase that really does justice to the changes is 'complete reconstruction'. The once really narrow, somewhat claustrophobic, tree-lined section had been a place to test the strongest nerves. However, the changes have not only produced a surface resembling that beloved of short-circuit racers, but have also completely opened out all the bends so that you can see right through the section as you approach it.

Now that fact itself is worth a couple of seconds off a lap time, elimination of the humps a couple more, while removal of the trees that funnelled you through the section has taken away another impediment. It is difficult to estimate the time-saving in total, but the section is now very fast. However, while the lesser lights might save as many as four seconds, the stars probably didn't worry; once more, it allows 'us' to get nearer 'their' lap times.

Now while the following Sulby Straight has always been straight, it is now flat, which it most certainly was not as recently as 1985. It was once so bumpy that riders of twin-shock machines bumped and weaved so badly that they rolled back the throttle for fear the bike would jump out of their hands. Sometimes, it did just that, and at top speeds. Thus, the changes saved the 'brave' little but, again, the 'mortals' quite a lot.

Sulby Bridge has been eased, the apex having been pulled back. It makes the corner that little bit faster and easier, saving probably another second.

Another jump that has almost disappeared from the circuit is that at Milntown Bridge. Once it produced yards of aviating and was a really daunting jump – the fastest men only just returned to earth in time to take the following right-hander. Now you only just leave the ground, which is an anti-climax after what it used to be. It certainly saves another second or two.

They will hardly change Parliament Square too much. However, while the essential shape of the swerving right/left must remain, nevertheless, it is inevitably smoother now, and the newcomer will be seen with his knee on the floor.

It is on the run up from the Gooseneck to Guthrie's Memorial that substantial resurfacing has taken place. Both my P&M RSC Honda and Suzuki Katana would jump about so much that I had to slow down because I could not see where I was going. Now, it is a smooth swerve from side to side

and a joy to ride through at full bore. It must have saved me at least 1.5 seconds.

Major changes have taken place at the Verandah, and while it looks very different with its marble-smooth surface, the actual contours have probably changed little, since all the opening out has taken place off the racing line. It still comprises four very fast corners, taken as one, but instead of worrying about bumps, you become concerned at just how far you are laying the bike over at something like 140 mph, well on my 1100 anyway.

The road surface down through Keppel Gate and Kate's Cottage used to be quite uneven enough to restrain the right wrist, but now it is possible to bore through and down towards the Creg, 'going for it', which should save another second.

Sweeping down through Hillberry is also something of a delight, where once the surface caused some concern. There is probably another second to be saved here. The total time saved is some 21 seconds, but that is not all. One of the principal improvements is the removal of much of the physical stress due to fighting the bike around the course, and in a six-lap race, doing it for over two hours.

Trying to estimate what all the changes have contributed to lap times is difficult. I would guess that my own saving, as a current midfield man, would be half a minute per lap, three minutes for a race.

16 The TT – a brief history

The races date from 1907, and they took place on the St Johns course before becoming established on the mountain circuit. From those early days and crude machines, the TT races achieved such a status that they were more important to manufacturers than winning world championships.

They were long regarded as the ultimate test for any machine; new models would appear there and disappear just as quickly, the rigours of the ruts, jumps and bumps wrecking frames and engines. However, those that survived the course did so with greatly enhanced sales potential. It was the shop

window of the British motorcycle industry, arguably perhaps, that of the world.

The nature of the course is changing – resurfacing proceeds apace, bends are eased and bumps are removed. Indeed, in my own competition career, the course has changed almost out of recognition, making possible speeds that would have been almost impossible, no matter how many bhp were 'on the end of the wire'.

In attempting a potted history of the world's most famous races, inevitably, one has to turn to the record books and past writings for information of the early days, and there is little better than Geoff Davidson's *The Story of the TT*, if you can find a copy. Geoff rode in the races of the 1920s, founding and editing the TT's own newspaper, which survived him and was published until 1987.

After taking part in some 80 races in the Island (by the time this book is published) and a stint at reporting the Manx Grand Prix for *The Special*, I trust that he, and everyone else whose records I have had to crib to write this guide, will bear with me. But facts are facts.

The TT began as a race for standard touring models, the name 'Tourist Trophy' following naturally. The races were staged in the Isle of Man because, at the time, the prevailing speed limit on mainland roads was just 20 mph. The Manx government, with the autonomy to pass their own Acts of Parliament to close public roads, were happy to make the event possible. In fact, there was already a precedent in that cars were already racing over 'our' mountain course.

However, the crude machines of the time, with their single gears and belt drives, were not thought to be capable of tackling the mountain, so a triangular track on the west side of the Island was used, taking in St Johns, Ballacraine, Kirk Michael and Peel. Not until 1911 did they take on the supreme test.

Those 80-odd years ago, machines were required to cover at least 90 miles per gallon if a single-cylinder machine, and 75 mpg if a twin. The race was ten laps of the 15.75-mile course, with an interval for lunch. Posterity records that a pedal-assisted, single-cylinder Matchless won, ridden by Charlie Collier. His speed was 38.23 mph and fuel consumption over 94 mpg. The winner of the twin-cylinder class was Rem Fowler on a Peugeot-engined Norton at 36.22 mph, although he did make the fastest lap of the race at 42.91 mph.

While bikes débuted on the mountain in 1911, it was not on the course as we know it. After the climb up from Hillberry, instead of turning left around Cronk-ny-Mona to Signpost, the course went straight on around the back of Douglas and joined the current course at the top of Bray Hill.

In those far-off days, the roads were scarcely 'metalled', except for the tarred section from Douglas to Ballacraine and a short stretch in Ramsey. Most of the tracks were simply compacted earth and stones, which would raise clouds of dust

when dry and be reduced to mud-filled potholes when wet. Until the 1920s, it would be a very fit rider who could stand at the end of a race.

The 'foreign' invasion of our racetracks is hardly a recent phenomenon, for in 1911 the race was won by an Indian ridden by O. C. Godfrey. This was also the year that a second race was staged in the programme, the Junior. It was won by P. J. Evans on a Humber twin.

Two-stroke race winners are not new either. A Scott took the laurels in 1912 and again in 1913, when the race distances were increased to six laps for the Juniors and seven for the Seniors. This was also the year when the races were held over two days, since riders needed time to recover between races. It was something of an interesting programme, though, in that the Juniors covered two laps in the morning, and the Seniors three in the afternoon. The next day, the survivors (75 per cent of the entrants) competed in one race with different coloured waistcoats to indicate whether they were Juniors or Seniors.

Crash helmets became compulsory wear in 1914, and with the race programme cut back to one day, Cyril Pullin won the Senior Race on a Rudge, and Eric Williams the Junior on an AJS. Then the 1914-18 war put a stop to racing for a while.

The races were resumed in 1920, the year when the course we know today was used, bringing in Signpost and Governor's. This year, a Lightweight Race also appeared in the programme, although the 250s were run with the Juniors. In fact, it was R. O. Clarke's 250 Levis that almost won outright, crashing just four miles from the finish. He still managed to get back on to win the class, however.

In that year Dunlop provided flag marshals to warn riders of obstructions in the road. This was because, in those days, the roads were not closed for practising; it was not until 1927 that this was done – a result of Archie Birkin crashing into a fish cart. His is the earliest fatality that seems to be on record.

The 1921 event was notable in producing one of those TT landmarks that are always quoted. It was the year that a Junior machine won the Senior race. The bike was an AJS ridden by Howard Davies, who was to go on to found the HRD marque.

For 1922 the Lightweight race received recognition, the 250 field being despatched ahead of the Juniors. It was also the year when the 1000th rider competed in the TT, although we do not have his name.

In 1923, a Sidecar Race was introduced, attracting just 14 entries. The most interesting machine technically was also the race winner. This was Freddie Dixon's 600 cc banking outfit. An ingenious device, operated by the passenger with a lever, allowed the whole outfit to lean in the required direction.

That it worked can be judged from the winning speed of over 53 mph, compared to the 55.5 mph winning speed of Sheard's 500 Douglas in the Senior Race, although the latter event was run in wet conditions.

They were still making changes to the programme in 1924 and, for the first time, five races were held, the addition being the 175 cc class. Race week assumed the familiar pattern of Monday, Wednesday and Friday. The Ultra-Lightweight race also made history in being the first to be mass-started, although there were only 17 starters. However, even the 175s averaged over 50 mph in the year when the course was lapped for the first time at over 60 mph. The credit went to the AJS ridden by Jimmy Simpson, who clocked over 63 mph from a standing start.

A couple of years later, in 1926, Simpson wrote his name in the record books once again when he lapped the TT course at over 70 mph in the Senior Race. By this time, the programme had been reduced to three main races; the poor entries in the Ultra-Lightweight and Sidecar classes had led to them being dropped. Jimmy Simpson needed only another five years to raise the lap record to 80 mph, this time riding a Norton. Not that the intervening years were without incident, but to mention every one would make this chapter longer than the rest of the book.

The years between the mid 1920s and late 1930s were the golden ones for British racing, with teams of factory machines from many camps fighting for the honours and the sales that victories inevitably brought. These were the days when legends were made by Simpson, Handley, Bennett, Walker, Dixon, Davies, Woods, Guthrie, Frith and many others too numerous to mention.

The year 1935 is worth recording as the year that the combined might of the British teams took a beating when Stanley Woods wheeled out the Italian Guzzis to clean up the Senior and 250 races, setting

a new lap record at 86.53 mph with the big Guzzi. However, Norton got back into their customary stride in the next two years with wins in Senior and Junior events. The winner of the 1937 Senior also established another milestone by putting in a lap at over 90 mph – the name in the record book was that of Freddie Frith, one of the greatest riders of the golden era.

In 1938 the lap record was raised to 91 mph by Senior winner Harold Daniel and was to stand for many years, in fact, until another legendary figure – Geoff Duke – came along in 1950. The previous year had seen the first introduction of evening practice, which set the style for subsequent events. These days, getting up in the dark at 4 am to go out and be early on the grid for practice is part of competing in the TT.

Amid the darkening war clouds of 1939, BMW were to score their only win, George Mier and Jock West with their supercharged power units proving far too quick for the Nortons. The latter were being run as 'privateers', for Norton were too involved in their efforts to make machines for the army's dispatch riders as war became inevitable.

After the war, as the world gradually regained its sanity, motorcycle racing became the pursuit of young men again. In 1947 the rules governing road racing were changed, supercharging being banned. This move nipped several promising new designs in the bud, while the dismal octane rating of the prevailing pool petrol brought engine power and speeds down.

The real innovation in 1947, however, was the introduction of the Clubmans TT in three classes: 1000, 500 and 350 cc. Rather like the Production races that were to follow in 1967, the regulations for the bikes required a certain number of machines to have been produced (25) and that those machines entered had lighting equipment and kickstarters. These Clubmans races were continued until 1956, by which time they were being dominated by BSA Gold Star machines, the resultant lack of interest killing them off.

Until 1950 the races carried on much as they had done in pre-war times, with the absence of a foreign challenge. Norton dominated the Senior races and did their best to oust Velocette from the Junior races. However, 1950 was the year when things started to change, as the old brigade that had spanned the war years began to retire and another of

racing's immortals – Geoff Duke – hit the top.

New boy to the Norton team, Geoff rewrote the record book with a lap at 93.33 on his way to winning the Senior, while Artie Bell, who had followed him home in the Senior, beat him on the smaller model to win the Junior. In 1951, though, he made a clean sweep with a double victory at speeds that no one could match. However, while the Italian factories had made the 250 class their playground for many years, the threatened challenge of the sophisticated four-cylinder 500s was looming. The writing was on the wall for the British singles, the design of which dated from the 1920s.

The multi-cylinder challenge from Italy was made real in 1952 when Les Graham took the big MV four to a second place in the Senior, behind Armstrong's Norton (Geoff Duke had suffered trouble), although not without experiencing oil leaks and a misfire. The fate of the British single was sealed, and it was only the brilliant riding of the Norton teamsters that was keeping the challenge of superior horsepower at bay.

Notable in 1954 was the controversial Senior race. Awarded to Norton's dashing Rhodesian rider, Ray Amm, the race was stopped due to inclement weather conditions while he was in front, Geoff Duke having just refuelled his Gilera. However, Norton wins in the Island were to become increasingly rare.

For 1954 it was the 250 race speeds that were making notable strides, the German NSU factory fielding a team with a brilliant new design that gave the winner, Haas, a 90 mph-plus winning speed.

1954 was the last year that Norton fielded a works team. Their attempts at streamlining to make the best of less-than-adequate horsepower are seen here with Ray Amm on the 'Anteater' or 'Proboscis' 500 Norton

It was just a little short of AJS-mounted Rod Coleman's Junior winning speed of 91.51 mph.

It was in 1954 that a new course was introduced, the Clypse course. Some ten miles long, it ran round the back of Onchan and was the venue for the reintroduced Sidecar and 125 races. In the following year, they were joined by the 250s and Clubmen. The course was dropped after 1959, though. While it was quite a challenging course in its own right, the mountain was felt to be proper TT racing.

The tens of thousands of enthusiasts watching the TT in 1955 were to hear it announced that the course had been lapped for the first time at over the magic 'ton', achieved by Geoff Duke when Gilera were at their race-winning best. However, it seems that the timekeepers changed their minds over the smallest part of a second, awarding him the fastest lap at 99.97 mph. Team-mate Armstrong took a second Arcore machine into the runner-up spot.

Meanwhile, in the same year, BMW had shattered the final Norton stronghold, the sidecar class, and were to establish a virtual monopoly for many years after. Geoff Duke was sidelined for the 1956 series, which saw MV score their first win in the hands of another master of the game, John Surtees.

Another milestone in the history of the TT came

First man to lap at over 100 mph, Bob McIntyre, seen here on his Joe Potts Norton, shows how to take Ballaugh – in level flight

about when Bob McIntyre broke the 'ton' in 1957, scoring a Senior/Junior double on Gileras. A temporary measure for that year was the stretching of the Senior race to a searching eight laps, but it didn't really prove or change anything, and the experiment was not to be repeated.

The seven-lap race of the following year saw Surtees dominate both Junior and Senior, MV being the only factory to field a full works team. Another experiment took place in the race programme in 1959 when the ACU introduced Formula classes, although they could hardly have guessed what was

to follow some years later. They were to last for one year only, being intended to keep out the Italian multis and give the home talent a chance to win a race. They were not to be repeated. McIntyre won the 500, and Alastaire King the 350.

All the races in the programme returned to the mountain course in 1960, the MVs continuing to dominate, but another milestone was passed when Derek Minter took a Norton round at over 101 mph. Hailwood also broke the 'ton' on his, while Surtees, in his Island swan-song, set the lap record at 104.08 mph on his way to another win.

Fate took a hand in 1961 when the MV of Gary Hocking struck trouble as Hailwood averaged over 100 mph to put Norton into the top spot for the last time in the Senior. In the Junior, luck struck again, slowing the MV sufficiently to give Phil Read a Norton victory. Another small piece of history was made when Tom Phillis rode a Norton Dominator-based racing twin to third place and notched a lap at over the 'ton' while doing so. It was also the year when the coming might of Honda made itself felt as 'Mike the Bike' scored his two other wins of that tremendous year in the 125 and 250 races.

Although 1962 might not be remembered for being outstanding in terms of TT history, it was the one year when BSA were to appear on the winner's rostrum, Chris Vincent having outlasted the BMWs to claim a surprise sidecar victory. In the big solo classes, Gary Hocking raised the lap record to 105.75 mph, while Hailwood hoisted the Junior record to 101.58 mph on the smaller of the MV fours. It also sticks in my own mind as being the first time I rode the mountain course.

In 1963 Mike pushed the record up to 106.41 mph in the Senior on the MV, but this was the year when Geoff Duke persuaded Gilera to take their 1957 bikes out of mothballs and staged a challenge to the mighty MV. That John Hartle managed to push the old Gilera round at over 105 mph was the highlight of the year, and he finished in second spot. For once, MV had to go for it, but then Mike always did. Meanwhile, Honda moved up to possess the Junior race, as Jim Redman, that most professional of professionals, took the honours.

For the next couple of years, the phenomenon that was Hailwood toured the MV in front of the field, but his performance in the very wet 1965 Senior is one still talked about by TT aficionados. Both MV's new boy, Giacomo Agostini, and Mike slid off at Sarah's Cottage. Mike, however, was able to kick his bike straight enough to ride back to the pits on three cylinders. After panic repairs, and with a carburettor jammed wide open, Mike went on to win the race.

For 1966 Mike signed up with Honda, and the bike that was to become the fastest round the TT course for many years made its appearance in the hands of the master. There was much speculation as to the horsepower of that bike – one figure quoted in the press was 114 bhp. Whatever the figure, it was

sufficient to give Mike the big victory, while Ago, who had been runner-up, won the Junior.

Mike had spent the season duelling with the growing two-stroke challenge in the 250 class around the Grands Prix, and having his hands very full, again showed his mastery of the course by setting a new quarter-litre record at 104.29 mph on his way to the rostrum.

While the rise of Honda met the MVs head-on, and the growing menace of the 'strokers' had provided the main interest at the TT for some years, in 1967 there were new races to 'delight' the enthusiast. The organizers introduced a Production Machine Race in three classes, similar to the original Clubmans races in 1947. The bikes were supposed to be 'over-the-counter' machines, only modified in the interests of safety. However, it was no ordinary factory Triumph Bonneville that John Hartle took to victory – it was capable of a timed 130 mph-plus.

This year also saw the epic Agostini/Hailwood duel in the Senior race when Mike set a speed of 108.77 mph. Mike was, perhaps, a little lucky when Ago's chain broke while he was just a 'gnats' in front. It left Mike to tour to his last victory for a decade, as Honda pulled out of Grand Prix racing at that time. For good measure, Mike made this year the second time he gained a trio of TT wins, taking the Junior with a record lap of 107.73 mph, and the 250 at 104.5 mph – speeds that stood for years.

It was little, but great, Bill Ivy's year in 1968. In winning the 250 race, he left the lap record at 105.51 mph on the bigger of his four-cylinder Yamahas, but it was his 100.32 mph lap on the 125 four that left everyone shaking their heads in disbelief as he practically rode around the walls. It was also my turn to set a lap record that was to stand for three years. I won the 500 cc Production Race at a speed of 91.03 mph on a Triumph Daytona which was clocked at 121.6 mph.

The years 1968-70 were when Agostini cruised the MV round to clean up the Senior and Junior races virtually unopposed. However, a milestone was passed when Malcolm Uphill recorded a lap at over 100 mph on a production bike – a Bonneville – while averaging 99.99 mph to win the 750 cc Production class.

Yet another new class appeared on the programme for 1971, this time for racing machines. These were based on a production power unit and

**Phil Read rounds
Waterworks Two on the
Yamaha 125 cc four in
the 1967 Lightweight
TT race. He won that
year at an average of
97.48 mph, with a
fastest lap at 98.36 mph**

**Fred Stevens at
Governor's Bridge in the
1967 Senior on a
Hannah Paton. He
scored fifth place in the
race, behind Hailwood,
Williams, Spencer and
Cooper** *(Nick Nicholls)*

conformed to Formula 750 specification, which the Auto Cycle Union was anxious to popularize as a means of bringing together American and Continental racing.

The Formula, to be accepted by the FIM, was similar to that of the American Motor Cycle Association. Tony Jefferies won the first race on a Triumph Trident, with a lap speed of 103.21 mph, while Ray Pickrell on the roadster version pushed the race average up to over 100 mph in winning the class, but not before Peter Williams notched a new record of 101.06 mph. Such was the famed reliability of the MV at the time that it is worth recording that Ago's Junior bike failed, allowing Tony Jefferies to win the Junior race, run in the very wet conditions that only the Island can arrange.

Also in 1971 a certain Barry Sheene made his Island début. He could so easily have become a friend of the TT, based on what the records show, rather than one who added fuel to the fire that ultimately led to its loss of Grand Prix status.

Starting No. 1 in the 125 race, he actually made the second fastest lap of the race before being caught by the experienced Charles Mortimer, who had started behind him.

In the book, *Will to Win*, Barry is quoted as following Chas over the mountain in rain and fog without knowing where he was going. Think what one may of the hazard of that action, but for sliding off at Quarter Bridge on his second lap, he surely would have been placed second and scored the World Championship points he sought. With those and good weather, he might well have taken a different view of things. It might even have taken some of the heat out of the controversy that was to surround the TT.

The 1972 event was notable only in that it was the last year that Giacomo was to parade the mighty MVs to victory, and that he did not make the fastest lap of the week. This singular honour went to Ray Pickrell, who won the 750 race at a speed of 105.68 mph. In fact, Ray was about three seconds faster on the Triumph triple than Ago was on the Senior triple.

However, the early 1970s were controversial years for the TT, as criticism mounted of the course and the meeting as a whole. Compared to other Grands Prix, it required a huge commitment of resources in time and money to compete as a top professional – a solid fortnight of machine wear and tear, hotel expenses, and the sheer aggravation of travelling to this far-flung corner of the racing world and setting up a racing workshop, something that was comparatively easy to do on the Continent. Talk of boycotts circulated in the paddock.

In performance terms, the 750s were beginning to make their mark as racing development of the BSA/Triumph triple and Norton Commando engines boosted performance. In 1973 Peter Williams finally earned his laurels with a win at

107.27 mph on the John Player Norton.

For 1974 a new race programme was announced that promoted the 750s to the Friday, the traditional highlight of the fortnight, and relegated the Senior to Wednesday. The 250, 350 and Senior races still carried World Championship status, but that was the last year they were to do so. The 750s were to be the jewel in the crown of the TT programme.

The 'crown' seemed to lack lustre, however, in a race week dogged by bad weather and re-scheduled races. What was now called the Open Formula 750 Classic was won by Chas Mortimer on a 350 Yamaha, at an average speed of just over 100 mph, only Percy Tait's Trident preventing complete two-stroke domination of the first eight places; the Senior was little better.

Real innovation appeared in 1975 in the shape of the ten-lap Handicap Race for Production machines. In the event, it proved to be something

of an interminable spectacle, and thoroughly confusing to watch, as bikes of all sizes droned by for hour after hour. The famous Trident, 'Slippery Sam', piloted by Dave Croxford and Alex George, scored a win in this somewhat sporadic procession.

In the following year, the ten-lapper was given one more try, but as a spectacle, it fared even worse than in the previous year, if that was possible. However, there was a highlight to the 1976 programme: the performance of Japanese star Takazumi Katayama. He brushed aside the perceived wisdom of the time which decreed that three years were necessary to learn the course, and on his first visit to the Island scored second in the 250 race to Tom Herron, and fourth in the Senior.

It was all-change again for 1977, as the TT Formula classes were introduced. These had three main objectives: to bring four-strokes back into the forefront of racing by specifying that engines be derived

RIGHT
1969 Lightweight TT, and here Kel Carruthers takes the entry to the Dip at Governor's Bridge on the works 250 Benelli (Nick Nicholls)

FAR RIGHT
A ten-lap Handicap Race took place in 1975 and 1976 for production machines of all classes. Here, the author is seen taking a Laverda Jota to third place in the 1000 cc class

from current production models; as a result of the foregoing, to encourage small manufacturers back into racing; and, perhaps most importantly, to regain a little of the Island's lost status in the racing world by applying the World Championship 'tag' to the classes. The last was thought to be an important factor in attracting visitors to the annual races.

Phil Read had been one of the most vociferous critics of the TT course, but he came back to the Island, it seemed with considerable alacrity, when Honda UK offered a contract that would revive his racing career. He was to ride a bored-out, 820 cc version of the 750 roadie motor in the Formula 1 Class. Even then, his win was rather controversial. In worsening weather conditions, Roger Nicholls, riding a Ducati in second place, had closed up to challenge, but he stopped for fuel on lap three. However, Honda waved Read through when he was about to do the same, and the race was stopped

on the next lap with the Honda in front.

This was also the year in which the 110 mph average fell, to Mick Grant in what was now called the Classic Race – for 750s. Meanwhile, Joey Dunlop scored the first of many victories by winning the Schweppes Jubilee race on the Friday. The poorly-supported Formula II Race had only eight finishers, while FIII had 13. About all they achieved were lots of lovely four-stroke noises through their open meggas.

When Mike Hailwood announced his comeback for the 1978 TT, enthusiasm in the Island knew no bounds, and many thousands more than usual flocked to watch the classic confrontation between Read, on the works Honda, and Mike on a Sports Motorcycles-entered Ducati. There was more than a touch of the 'David and Goliath' about it. Read – on the more powerful four – was the bad boy who had 'rubbished' the TT, while 'Mike the Bike', with

his gentlemanly persona, was dubbed the Greatest. His Italian V-twin was considerably slower.

The race itself has been chronicled many times elsewhere. Mike won, and although Read did not finish, he was beaten anyway. As a race, it was outstanding, but, above all else, it was to breathe new life into the TT, and the Island's coffers benefited accordingly. As a result, more money could be pumped into supporting the races.

A year later, Mike's Ducati was not the bike it had been in that F1 race, but on a Suzuki team bike built from spares, he surpassed himself by setting a new lap record at 114.02 mph while on his way to winning the Senior. In the Schweppes Classic race, another notable duel was played out between Alex George and Mike. The two were never more than seconds apart, but George wrung extra revs from the 998 F1 Honda to shade Mike across the line by 2.5 seconds.

With Mike having finally retired, the TT had new names and a new record to carry the races forward in 1980. Graeme Crosby won the Senior and just failed to catch Mick Grant in the F1 event, while Joey Dunlop hoisted the lap record to 115.22 mph in winning the Classic.

The races were certainly holding their popularity with competitors – the home-brew of new talent still regarded it as the supreme challenge for 1981, and there was a record number of entries. An ACU selection panel had to reduce the numbers, finally accepting reserves for some races. Of a total of 638 race entries for the eight races, no less than 112 were for the Senior.

In 1981 Historic machines appeared in the TT programme for the first time, and they have continued to be a regular and popular feature of the fortnight ever since. They were given a two-lap cavalcade, with many of the stars from yesteryear riding the same machines on which they made TT history. On a personal note, it was also the year when I finally topped the 'ton' after many near misses.

I confess to having neglected the 'chair' brigade, but it is the consequence of cramming 80 years of history into one chapter. However, chairs made news this year when Jock Taylor inscribed an incredible speed of 108.12 mph in the record books on his way to winning the first leg of the three-wheeler race.

The official results for 1983 note that race records

were broken in four classes and that the course record was also broken. This milestone went to Norman Brown in a time of 19 minutes, 29 seconds at an average speed of 116.19 mph in the Senior Classic before he retired in the third lap. Rob McElnea scored the win on the 997 F1 Suzuki.

Two changes took place to the programme in 1984: the introduction of a three-lap race for Historic machines and of a Production race; the programme featured nine races. This year also saw Joey Dunlop push the outright lap record to 118.47 mph in the Senior, and American Dave Roper win the Historic race; even scored fourth myself – on a Triumph.

It was back to a seven-race programme for the next year. The Historic race was not repeated, and while there were no milestones, Joey had an F1, Senior and Junior triple; he was fast becoming 'Mr TT'. By 1986, many were of the opinion that there was too much Production racing. There were now four classes and two races, the machines packing the grid wherever competitors could obtain another ride.

Fate decreed awful weather for 1987. The Senior was reduced to four laps in very heavy rain, about the only time I have seen full wet tyres used. Competitors pulled out in droves, myself included. Even then, it was postponed and run on the Saturday, while the combined Production race for 1300s and 600s was cancelled. Joey scored two more, with Senior and F1 wins. While Production machines still packed the programme, coming in for more criticism, it was notable that the 750s provided one of the best races of the week, the first six averaging over 109 mph.

The year 1988 saw yet another hike in the ultimate lap record as Steve Cull took a Honda RS500 three-cylinder two-stroke round at a fraction over 19 minutes – in fact, just 0.6 second – resulting in a lap at 119.08 mph. Sadly, the bike burst into flames on the last lap, and Joey Dunlop inscribed yet another win in the record book. Indeed, he did so in the F1, and went on to complete yet another triple by annexing the Junior as well. 'Signposts' for the year were Geoff Johnson's lap at 116.55 mph on a Production 1000 Yamaha, and a fraction off 113 mph on the 750; in fact, 112.98 mph with a lap at 20 minutes, 2.2 seconds. These speeds by Production bikes were receiving mixed comment. The detractors of the classes saw them as being boring and monopolizing the programme to the detriment of the 'proper' races, while supporters saw them as the future of the TT.

The following year, 1989, was also significant for the TT, and it saw another U-turn in the programme. This was prompted by five competitor fatalities and the need for the organizers to be seen to be doing something to restrain the mounting speeds in the interests of safety. Production bikes took the brunt of the furore that resulted from media coverage of a sensational nature, largely in *Motor Cycle News*, where one might have expected support.

In this one year, Hislop took on the mantle of 'Mr TT', as he won three races. The first of these was the Supersport 600 class, which was rapidly gaining in popularity, having been introduced in the European Championships. With machine specifications regulated to reasonably standard engines, it was a staggering achievement to win on a Honda CBR at an average of 112.58 mph, although the fastest lap went to the Yamaha of Dave Leach at 113.60 mph. Steve completed his triple by winning the Senior and F1 races.

Thus, the programme that was announced for 1990 contained no Production races at all – the wheel had turned almost full circle. The 1300 cc limit that had prevailed for the Senior race was reduced to 750 cc, a restriction that was also applied by the Manx Grand Prix organizers.

Perhaps ironically, it was the Honda RC30 that was the F1 race winner and monopolizer of the class, with its look-alike production road-going equivalent, that allowed Steve Hislop to set a speed that was a fraction short of 122 mph for a lap in practice. In fact, he *only* clocked 121.34 mph in winning the race; just 18 minutes, 39.4 seconds to cover the 37.7 miles.

Steve Hislop's luck deserted him in 1990; his second place in the Junior would have been enough to please many, but with his record, it seemed like disaster. Sure enough, he was the fastest man of the week in practice, which had not been blessed with the best weather. Actually, he took just 18 minutes, 44 seconds on the Wednesday evening to record 120.84 mph to top the F1 class.

However, it was Carl Fogarty who took the win in the F1 class, recording an average of 118.35 mph. Steve had a protracted pitstop, after which he recorded fastest lap of the race at 18 minutes, 27.6

seconds (122.63 mph) and finished in ninth place. With Honda taking the win with their RC30. Nick Jeffreys had maintained station all the way through on the Yamaha OW01, and it was nice to see Norton come good as Robert Dunlop brought the 588 RCW rotary on to the rostrum.

The combined 400 and 125 race provided Dunlop the younger with a win as he coaxed his tiny Honda home to an incredible 103.41 mph average, with a fastest lap at 104.09 mph. The 400s really seemed to have made their mark in the programme, as new four-cylinder machines from Yamaha, Kawasaki and Honda fought for honours. The winner, Dave Leach, on an FZR Yamaha, scorched round at 109.39 mph, only seconds in front of second place-man Fogarty on a V4 Honda VFR.

A titanic battle took place in the Junior event between Ian Lougher (Yamaha) and Steve Hislop (Honda). They were never more than a few seconds apart, but Hislop, who had led until lap four, lost a precious second or so in his pitstop, allowing Lougher to win by just two. Lougher's fastest lap, at a little short of 118 mph, and his race average of 115.16 mph would put many 750s to shame.

With the Sidecar class capacity limit being reduced this year to the same as that of Formula II – 350 cc for two-strokes and 600 cc for four-strokes – it was gratifying to see the ultimate three-wheeler lap record holder, Mick Boddice, mount a challenge to the two-strokes with a CBR Honda-engined outfit. True, Dave Saville's Sabre Yamaha was never seriously threatened, but it bodes well for the class, as Boddice averaged over 100 mph in both races.

When the 1991 programme was announced, the excellent performances of the 125s and 400s had been rewarded, as they were given four laps to race over. The need for extra practice had also been recognized, as there was no longer a race on Friday night.

The story continues and the programme evolves to take account of new machine trends, and the commercial and safety lobbies. Perhaps what grows even more is the whole programme of supporting events that make up a fortnight's cavalcade of motorcycle sport which is unequalled anywhere else in the world. Some would say that the sum of the parts now exceeds the whole of the programme, certainly of the races themselves. In fact, if the races are ever stopped, the festival itself might well carry on in its own right.

17 The Manx Grand Prix

The Manx Grand Prix is quite incredible in that entries continue to rise every year and are frequently over-subscribed. Yet, in these hard commercial times, there is not one penny of prize money. Truly have the races been called the Amateur TT.

It is the magic lure of the mountain course that induces riders to pay, at 1988 prices £70 just to enter a race. There is little trade support, unlike the TT. The Steam Packet Ferry fare can easily cost over £200, there will be tyres to buy, as well as fuel, and unless you camp in the paddock, a fortnight's accommodation, in a boarding house or hotel, will really hurt an impecunious racer's budget.

Yet even in the Classic events, riders are turned away every year. Fortunately, the spirit that launched the races back in 1923 still prevails and led to the organizers bringing in a Newcomers Race in 1957 and 1958, although the current series of Newcomers events was started in 1978. They are the nursery for both the 'Prix' and the TT. Riders with a long-term view of their career will use them as stepping stones to the international races and, perhaps, to fame and fortune. However, even today, I don't think too many have achieved that from racing.

The Manx Grand Prix was the brainchild of the Manx Motor Cycle Club, which was formed in

RIGHT
For the first ever try at the mountain, the author built this 500 Royal Enfield engine into a 7R AJS frame of 1948 vintage. It was capable of nearly 100 mph downhill. After being soaked and frozen, getting lost on the mountain and stopping on the last lap to warm up, he finished 56th and last but one

FAR RIGHT
This was the pit lane for the 1988 Manx Grand Prix. Note the lines to impose a traffic discipline on racers for safety's sake

1912. For many years it ran reliability trials and speed competitions, but in 1923 events conspired to make them initiate what is probably the second most popular race in the UK racer's calendar.

In fact, the origins of 'The Manx' lay in the events of 1921 when the Auto Cycle Union was approached by the government of Belgium who wanted them to stage the TT races in that country. Nevertheless, the following year's TT races were held, as usual, on the mountain circuit, but the establishment in the island had been shaken by the thought of losing a major tourist attraction and a potential replacement was seen to be desirable.

Another factor was that the TT was clearly an event in which anyone lacking a fair measure of trade support stood little chance. The feeling among members of the Manx MCC was that something ought to be done to redress the balance and give the amateur a chance to win an award over the toughest course of all. The concept of an 'amateur TT' was born, christened the Manx Amateur Road Races.

That first race in 1923 enjoyed a 33-strong grid and was won by a certain Les Randles on a Sunbeam at an average speed of 52.77 mph. Both 350 and 500 cc classes were run together, and the race was of five laps. However, it was the definition of 'amateur' that caused trouble in those days.

The term was defined thus: 'one who, at the time of making an entry, was not, nor had not been, engaged in the manufacture for sale, or the sale or repair, or the exhibition of cars or motorcycles, their parts and accessories.' In spite of that definition, after the 1929 races, there were allegations in the *Isle of Man Times* that bonuses had been paid to riders. Consequently, for 1930, simpler rules were drawn up. Entries continued to rise and reached 101 for what had become two separate class races, introduced in 1928.

For 1934, a 250 class race was introduced into the programme; previously, the 250s had raced with the 350s. The class was to stay in the programme until 1949 when lack of suitable competitive machinery caused the organizers to drop it. However, it returned in 1964.

By 1957 the popularity of the Manx had reached

staggering proportions, more entries being returned than it was possible to accept – the grid for each race was 100. Therefore, a Newcomers Race was introduced, for which no less than 380 entries were received; only 118 places were available in the programme. The idea was that finishers would be rewarded with a place on the grid for the 'Prix' proper. In essence, it was a sort of elimination race.

Repeated in 1958, the race produced another rush of newcomers wanting to make their début on the world's most famous circuit. In some ways, rather than solving the problem of having too many entrants for the main races, the race served merely to compound this difficulty. For although the races were intended to serve as a nursery for those aspiring to greater things in the TT, most riders wanted to stay with the Manx and entries continued to be overwhelming.

A further problem, however, was simply that of getting the 400-odd marshals to turn out for an extra day. Reversion to the original programme followed in 1959 when entry acceptance returned to the system that provided a balance between current good performances by established men and newcomers with a good record on the short circuits.

I well remember one of the great landmarks of the Manx being established in 1973 when I had been enrolled as a reporter for the *Manx Grand Prix Special* newspaper. Sitting in the grandstand's press box, listening to the Manx Radio commentary, I recorded my own impressions of the race, culled from the commentary and the activity taking place in front of me in the pits. Phil Haslam broke the 100 mph barrier for the race and rewrote the record books with a speed of 103.15 mph on his way to winning the Junior race. He just missed a 100 mph average for the race. The atmosphere really was electric as the announcement was made. The whole grandstand gasped to a man, if that was possible, and carried on discussing it for the rest of the race.

With the three-race programme of 250, 350 and 500 running again from 1964, the next change in race format came in 1978 when a Newcomers Race featured again, combining Senior, Junior and Lightweight clases. A certain Ron McElnea scored second in the Junior class. Later, like many another Grand Prix star, he was to go on to contest world championships with a works team.

While a multitude of talented riders made their names in the races in the intervening period, it was

The author at the Gooseneck during the 1963 Manx. The bike is a 500 unit Triumph motor fitted into a Triumph Twenty-One frame. It steered erratically and lost some gears, but finished 32nd; lapped at 83 mph

in 1988 that Phil Hogg cracked another of those intervals on the clock that the press never cease to describe as 'barriers'. He went round in under 20 minutes in the Senior race – 19 minutes, 51.2 seconds, for a speed of 114.02 mph. The race was won at over 110 mph by Paul Hunt.

Truly, the Manx has fulfilled the purpose of its founders, and many famous names have established themselves in the September races to go on to greater things. Among them are Freddie Frith, Geoff Duke and Phil Read, all of whom became world champions.

18 Andreas and Jurby

The fact that the Manx Grand Prix attained National competition status in 1967 posed problems for resident Isle of Man racers starting out on their competition careers. It was to have far-reaching consequences, the first of which was that it simply was no longer possible for locals to tackle the mountain circuit before they had earned their National competition licences.

The result was that novices had to travel to the mainland to compete in their first race in a club event, something of a deterrent to making any start in competition. The situation was seen as such a potential threat to the development of Manx road-racing talent that it led to the formation of the Andreas Racing Association as a nursery of local riders.

It was actually in 1968 that Air Vice Marshal, the Reverend Patterson-Fraser became founder President of the association and, at the time of writing, he still held that position. A circuit was laid out on Andreas Airfield, but permission for its use was withdrawn just before the first meeting was due to be run.

However, the first meeting to take place under the association's banner was in April 1970, on a road course at Jurby, which is still used today. On the morning of that inaugural meeting, there was snow on the course, and club secretary Norman Cowan recollects the apprehension felt by all before it cleared in time for practice to take place.

Two meetings a year were held on this course, right through to 1987; for 1988 the association succeeded in obtaining three road closure orders, bearing witness to the support that the races have in the House of Key. Indeed, so does all racing in the Isle of Man. Clearly, it would not survive without such support.

Noel Clegg won the first solo race, and John Worthington the three-wheeler class, and it was a three-wheeler, too – something he called a Scitsu!

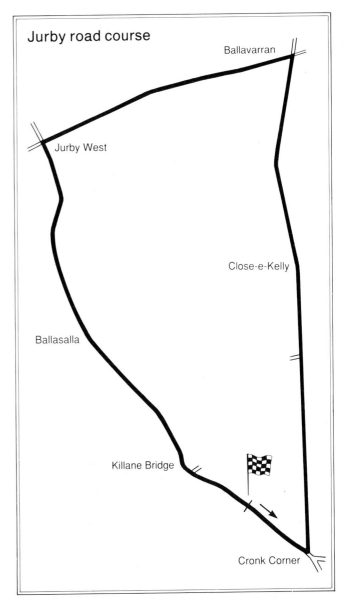

Jurby road course

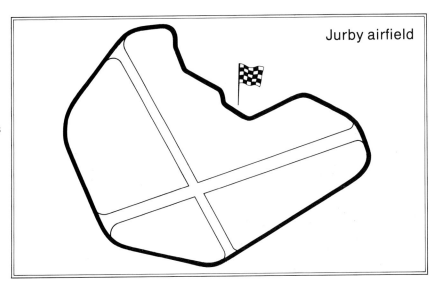

Jurby airfield

LEFT
A real vintage-looking chair with George Oates and Gorden Garrett at Killane Bridge. They do not build them like that anymore

BELOW LEFT
Cronk corner on the road circuit in 1975; Tom Christian leads on his Aermacchi

Danny Shimmin was the 1300 cc winner, while Richard Fitzsimmons won the 250 on a Suzuki that he still campaigns to this day in Classic events.

It was in 1974 that races were first staged on Jurby Airfield. A practice day was held in April to get the feel of things, while the first airport race meeting was run immediately after the Southern 100 meeting to catch some of the competitors before they departed the Island. That year, the two road and a further two airport meetings really gave the association a race programme to be proud of. That they have a friend in high places can be seen from the fact that this was the year that David Cretny rode, and he is now a member of the House of Keys.

In 1976 the famous Welshman Gordon Pantel put the record for the road course up to 103 mph. That was also the year when the first National permit was granted for the meeting. Names that were on their way to becoming established made places for themselves in the record books as the years went by, and in 1977 it was Kevin Wilson (then living in Onchan), George Fogarty and Joey 'Yer Maun' Dunlop who broke lap records. The speeds are amazing when considered in the light of the 14 ft width of the roads in some places and 4.25-mile length of the course.

'King' Kenny Harrison rode in 1978 to record an astonishing 21 wins out of 22 starts, while the following year saw the introduction of the Celtic Match Races. These were devised as part of the Tynwald Millenium event, the 1000th anniversary

of the Manx Parliament, and they proved to be a very hard-fought series between the Irish and the Scots. This was the year when there were no less than five Keen brothers on the startline: Mike, Norman, Richard, Phil and Kenny.

In 1980 the Oates brothers became sidecar champions on the 2.14-mile airport circuit at a 74 mph race speed. This course variation was very twisty and included the perimeter track and the road round the hangers. This last section has since been lost due to the workshops that are there now, but three courses are still contrived so that riders can qualify for their licences by having ridden on three different tracks.

One of the interesting things about the association and its 200-odd members is that each rider has to take a turn at marshalling. It is the only way that they can obtain the full complement of officials needed to stage a meeting, and any rider not prepared to do his bit would have his entry refused. Sadly, such a system probably would not work on the mainland where there are so many clubs and meetings for riders to choose from.

The road circuit record of 107.9 mph still stood at the time of writing, set in 1983 by Kenny Harrison. Lowry Burton won the 'chairs' at 98.2 mph that year. The association continued to run a busy season through to 1988 when a couple of sprint meetings were staged for good measure, and a further six were scheduled for 1989.

19 The Billown circuit

Racing started on the 4.25-mile Billown circuit in 1955, the intention being to provide local clubmen with some road-racing experience before tackling the Manx Grand Prix. The club staging the races was the Southern Motor Cycle Club, an organization much concerned with trials and scrambles, but later a separate body was set up purely to stage the races: the Southern 100 Motor Cycle Racing Club. The Southern 100 takes its name from the original length of the main race at 24 laps. The club also stages the Classic TT races under the auspices of the ACU.

However, from its inception as a three-race event to the present day with its ten-race programme and match-race series, the S100 has provided the keenest competition among some of the best-known names in UK racing. It has even attracted visiting 'colonials' to its bumpy, and still largely original, public roads.

Many of the happy band who started the club when the races were first staged all those years ago are still associated with it, and it is now a highly-respected meeting in July. Indeed, some, like Phil Taubman, Norman Gill and Theo Watterson, can still be seen in the programme as serving official positions. In fact, Phil is a very busy Clerk of the Course who looks forward to many more years 'in harness'.

Manxman Derek Ennett was the first winner of the Junior Race, and on one of the fast, but fragile, G45 Matchless pushrod twins was contesting the lead in the Senior, behind eventual winner Terry Shepherd on a Norton, when gremlins relegated him to third place behind Alastair King.

Many other famous names have featured in the S100 record books, even before it gained National status in 1958, when the meeting was first held over two days. It was the scene of a titanic battle between regular winner Alan Shepherd and famous Scot Bob McIntyre. Shepherd made it for a third Senior win.

In the Senior race of the following year, 'Bob Mac' actually won – but then lost it, as he was disqualified for refuelling, which was not allowed under the regulations. Ron Langston, who had diced hard with McIntyre in the early stages, was pronounced the winner.

For 1961, a four-race programme was introduced, the 125s taking their place on the grid. Another of the great names from the past, Dan Shorey, wrote his name in the record books with a win. In that year, Phil Read won the big one and dead-heated the Junior with Alan Shepherd, while John Hartle fielded a Honda four to win the Lightweight 250 class.

Read continued his winning ways in 1962 with a Senior/Junior double, and while that was a cracking performance for a rider making his way in the game, just as impressive was Arthur Wheeler who, at the age of 42, cleaned up the 250 race on his ten-year-old Moto Guzzi, setting a new race record in the process. At the time of writing (early 1989), he was still riding basically the same machine in the Classic Manx Grand Prix and putting up very creditable performances. The programme was completed in 1962 by a race for chairs, Charlie Freeman being the winner on his Norton.

Famous names continued to feature every year as the meeting continued to grow in stature, among them being such stars of the decade as Selwyn Griffiths and Brian Steenson. In 1968 the Solo Championship was introduced, the first 15 riders from the previous three races being qualified to ride; Steve Jolly was the winner.

By 1970 the big race was given a 750 cc limit, although it was won by Brian Adams on a 500 Norton. Chair races opened and closed the race programme. In the big race of the 1972 programme, Bill Smith took his Honda four 'under the linen' first.

The 1975 event saw the first 90 mph laps, Ray

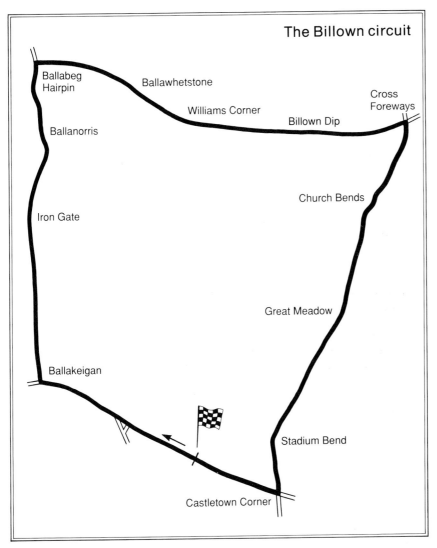

The Billown circuit

Ballabeg Hairpin
Ballawhetstone
Williams Corner
Billown Dip
Cross Foreways
Ballanorris
Church Bends
Iron Gate
Great Meadow
Ballakeigan
Stadium Bend
Castletown Corner

McCullough being the first to turn in this speed on a Yamaha 350, while a 1000 cc race was also added to the programme. It was won by local rider Danny Shimmin on a 700 Yamaha. The next year was the first that Joey 'Yer Maun' Dunlop made his first appearance, scoring second place in the 750 race behind Bill Smith. By then, Bill was being referred to as a veteran. He won the Championship race, setting new lap and race records (the fastest lap was 94.09 mph in a time of 2 minutes, 42.6 seconds), on a Yamsel – a 350 Yamaha motor housed in a Colin Seeley frame.

Dunlop established a dominance of the races in 1977 and 1978, but in 1979 he was both unlucky and lucky. Firstly, he had to stop at Castletown Corner to remove tape from the radiator, as it was causing the motor to overheat. Then, at Ballanorris, while speeding between the dry stone walls, the steering damper jammed, but Joey was able to wrestle the bike into a field through a gate that is left open at that point for just such an eventuality. George Fogarty scored the win.

The 25th anniversary of the meeting occurred in 1979. Now, a decade on, the big names continue to write their names in the results: riders like Con Law, Brian Reid, Kenny Harrison and Lowry

RIGHT
Sidecars line up for the first bend after the start, Ballakeigan, a sharp right leading into the downhill straight to the Iron Gate

FAR RIGHT
Solos squabble round Ballabeg; the Billown really is a tight road circuit

Burton. Prize money, too, has kept up with the times, and in 1989 there was some £4000 on offer to make sure the big names were attracted to the meeting, which is scarcely equalled for the camaraderie of the officials and the keenness of the competiton.

The start is on the wide open and smooth-surfaced Castletown-Port St Mary/Port Erin main road. Competitors reach the paddock and startline via the back road through Castletown itself, then go out again towards St Mary.

The first corner is Ballakeigan, a second- or third-gear corner, with fairly high gearing, but it is the one that really sorts out the pack, having a difficult approach that the brave can take advantage of. It is something like half a mile from the start and has a slightly curving right and left uphill.

Downhill now and going hard, the Iron Gate section is an S-bend over a bridge that can be taken very fast, but it is not a place for the faint-hearted. There is no room for error, and the surrounding high stone walls are most daunting at first acquaintance.

After accelerating out of the Iron Bridge's left-hander over the railway, the road still goes left through Ballanorris, just a left-hander that, taken with real bottle, can be going hard, *but* only when you really know it. The open gate is the only escape route, as Joey Dunlop can testify.

Ballabeg Hairpin is not a hairpin in the true sense, but it is certainly acute. It is probably around 110 degrees, going right, and leads into a section that preserves a real impression of what the mountain circuit once was, before all the changes.

The mile through to Cross Four-ways is very bumpy and uneven enough to make newcomers to the course ease off. The swerve left/right that is Ballawhetstone is compounded by steep cambers and is best taken in true Island style, peeling off late and driving out hard.

Climbing up a rise, the road seems to curve left at William's Corner, but if you can stop the bike drifting down the camber as you breast the rise, there is a lot of time to be made here. Then comes the run down to the Crossways and a very severe test of brakes.

At this point, having covered three miles, it is very hard right for the mile down to Castletown Corner, then a short squirt followed by Church Bends, which have been resurfaced and are now smooth. They are quite sharp, however, being right/left, and very scratchy with high walls on each side. Next, there is the top-speed run through Great Meadow, then the flat-out left curve, Stadium Bend, before Castletown Corner's very sharp right.

With little more than 100 yd to go before the Start/Finish line, Castletown Corner is where races are won and lost in last-minute braking while still heeled over from Stadium Bend. The corner itself is quite awkward, being very sharp indeed. Here there is a slim chance of a slipstreaming manoeuvre to improve your position in the run to the Finish.

The Billown circuit is really a square; four principal sharp corners with swerves in between. Its bumps will sort out deficiencies in suspension, and brakes will be really tested. Gearing will need to be quite high, perhaps just a tooth or two down on that for the mountain course.

20 The Clypse course

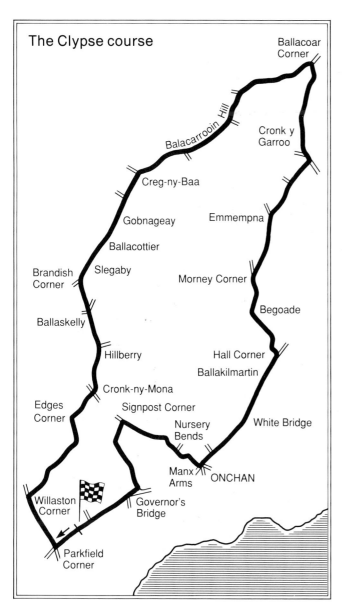

The Clypse course

Ballacoar Corner
Balacarrooin Hill
Cronk y Garroo
Balacarrooin Hill
Creg-ny-Baa
Gobnageay
Emmempna
Ballacottier
Brandish Corner
Slegaby
Morney Corner
Ballaskelly
Begoade
Hillberry
Hall Corner
Ballakilmartin
Cronk-ny-Mona
Edges Corner
Signpost Corner
White Bridge
Nursery Bends
Manx Arms
ONCHAN
Willaston Corner
Governor's Bridge
Parkfield Corner

The first race meeting on the 10.97-mile Clypse circuit took place in 1954, after which the course was used for a further five years, until 1959. By then the increasing speeds and factory interest in the smaller solo classes led to the latter, together with the sidecars, returning to the supreme challenge of the mountain circuit.

The first-ever winner on the course was Rupert Hollaus, who took his 125 cc NSU to victory, while that 'great' of three-wheel fame, Eric Oliver, won the 'chair' race on a Norton; the speeds were 69.57 and 68.87 mph respectively.

The circuit was deemed a success, and for 1955 the 250s were 'relegated' to the Clypse course, although at over ten miles in length, it was still longer, and certainly more arduous, than most circuits anywhere in the world. Bill Lomas scored the first 250 win on an MV, while another superb rider from yesteryear, Carlo Ubbiali, made it a double for MV on the little one. It fell to Walter Schneider to annex the 'chair' race, which BMW would dominate henceforth.

In 1956 Ubbiali gave MV the double, although he was to share the honours with Tarquinio Provini through to 1959 in the Lightweight class. Only Cecil Sandford was able to split the pair, in 1957, when he piloted a 250 Mondial to the top spot.

For the circuit's last year, the records stood in perpetuity to Provini's MVs at 77.77 and 74.06 mph. Schneider left the three-wheel score at 73.01 mph in winning the 1958 race; his 1959 time was just a little slower. After this, all classes went back to 'proper' TT racing.

The circuit itself was really a very interesting and testing track. It started at the familiar TT grandstand, but turned immediately right at the crossroads, then carried on along Ballanard Road to Willaston Corner, where it went right again. This led the track to join the TT course, but in the reverse direction, at Cronk ny Mona.

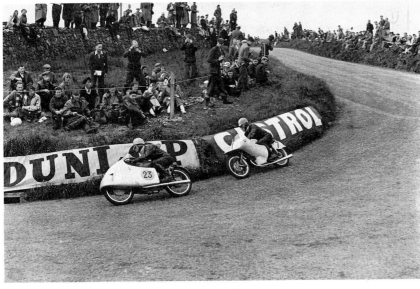

ABOVE LEFT
Eric Oliver – a legendary
sidecar racer who kept
Norton in front long
after they had lost the
power struggle to BMW
– rounds a bend on the
Clypse

LEFT
Ubbiali, no. 23, on a 125
MV, leads R. Hollause
on the NSU

Racing now in the 'wrong' direction, riders on the Clypse followed the mountain course up to Creg ny Baa, where it turned right and positively wound its way up Ballacarrooin Hill. This was real Isle of Man going, the road being little wider than a track and very bumpy at racing speeds.

At the 5.5-mile point, reaching Ballacoar Corner, the road went hard right, twisted down to Cronk ny Garro, through Morney Corner and down to Hall Corner, and then joined the Onchan-Laxey main road. The course went on into Onchan village, turning right at the Manx Arms and up to Signpost Corner to join the TT circuit again. Finally, the course followed the mountain road down to Governor's and back to the start/finish.

It certainly was a testing circuit in the best traditions of the Island, and one only has to ride round it now to appreciate what a near 80 mph average meant on those roads.

21 A personal Isle of Man record

Manx Grand Prix

Year		Machine	Result	F/laps	Replica	Remarks
1962	Senior	'Redplum'	56th	30.15 = 75 mph	0	Very wet, stopped on 5th lap—restarted
1963	Senior	Hughes/Triumph	32nd	27.19 = 83 mph	0	Lost 3rd gear
	Junior	,,	49th	27.30 = 82.3 mph	0	
1964	Senior	Hughes/Triumph	Rtd	25.45 = 87.92 mph	0	Oil tank split
	Junior	,,	Rtd	—	0	Ignition failed
1965	Senior	Hughes/Triumph	Rtd	25.27 = 89 mph	0	Coil wire broke lap 1, battery flat lap 2
1966	Senior	Hughes/Triumph	30th	82 mph ave.	0	Battery flat, engine missing
	Junior	,,	24th	27.21	0	Won team prize with Ron Baily & A. Peck
1985	Classic	RSM/Triumph	10th	87.11 mph ave.	Rep	Naylor Trophy – wet!
1986	Classic	RSM/Triumph	14th	25.06 = 90 mph	Rep	Naylor Trophy – 89.93
1987	Classic	RSM/Triumph	15th	25.06 = 90 mph	0	
1988	Classic	RSM/Triumph	Rtd			

TT Races

Year		Machine	Result	F/laps	Replica	Remarks
1967	Prod	650	Rtd	—	0	Holed piston lap 1
	Senior	Triumph	27th	26.07 = 86.7 mph	Bronze	(Hailwood won)
	Junior	Hughes/Triumph	30th	26.41 = 84.8 mph	Bronze	
1968	Prod	Daytona	FIRST	24.52 = 91.03 mph	Silver	Lap & race records, won £50!
	Senior	,,	Rtd	25.33	0	Broke rod
	Junior	Hughes/Triumph	Rtd	26.26	0	
1969	Prod	Daytona	2nd	25.37	Silver	to G. Penny CB440
	Senior	Hughes/Triumph	30th	25.48	0	Last lap 1 cylinder
	Junior	,,	Rtd	—	0	4th lap Glentramman

Year		Machine	Result	F/laps		Replica	Remarks
1970	Prod	Daytona	3rd	25.02		Silver	to Whitway/Pantell
	Senior	CRD/Triumph	Rtd	—		o	Oil leak r/counter
	Junior	Hughes/Triumph	Rtd	—		o	Blew at Highlander
	L/Wt	Ducati	29th	79 mph		Bronze	Prod Ducati
1971	F750	Trident	11th	24.59		Silver	Bad handling
	Prod	Daytona	Rtd	25.27		o	Points closed
	Senior	Hughes/Triumph	Rtd	—		o	Battery flat
1972	Prod	Daytona	4th	25.03		Silver	
	F750	Trident	14th	24.31 = 92.0 mph		Silver	
	Senior	Daytona	Rtd	25.48		o	Engine
1973	Prod	Daytona	7th	26.01		Silver	
	F750	Trident	27th	23.33		Silver	
	Senior	RSM/Triumph	Rtd	—		o	Crank lap 1
1974	Prod	Trident	Rtd	—		o	Broke rod lap 1
	F750	Honda	Rtd	—		o	Crash Braddan Bridge
	Senior	RSM/Triumph	28th	26.00		o	Wet!
1975	Prod 10-lap Handicap						
		Daryn/BMW90S	7th	24.01		o	with Alan Walsh
			21st o/a				

A win in the 500 cc class of the 1968 Production race. There were only 14 entered for the class. John Blanchard on a works Velo was second, and Dave Nixon on a Boyer Triumph third

Winning trio after the 1968 Proddy race, left to right: Ray Pickrell, who won the 750 class on a Dunstall Dominator, the author, and Trevor Burgess, who won the 250 class on an Ossa

Year		Machine	Result	F/laps	Replica	Remarks
1976	Prod 10-lap Handicap					
		Slater/Jota	3rd 19th o/a	23.12 = 97 mph	Silver	with Mick Hunt
1977	F1	Dresda/Honda	13th	24.02	Bronze	Wet, reduced to 4 laps
1978	F2	Honda	Rtd	—	o	Head gasket 1 lap
	F1	Dresda/Honda	13th	22.42 = 99 mph	Silver	(Hailwood won!)
1979	F2	Honda	8th	24.03	Bronze	£85
	F1	CB-900	22nd	22.54	o	Crash Governor's
1980	F1	Honda	30th	23.37	o	Steering disaster
	F2	Laverda 500	14th	25.57	o	Wettish
	Senior	Luke/Honda	31st	23.45	o	
	Classic	Honda	Rtd	—	o	Wet plugs
1981	F1	Brett/Honda	Rtd	22.34 = 100 mph	o	Clip-on broke lap 4
	F2	,,	17th	23.12	o	Lost 7 minutes, push-in
1982	F1	Suzy Katana	20th	22.54	o	
	F2	Yamaha	Rtd	—	o	Seized 3 ×
1983	F1	P & M/Honda	18th	22.03 = 102 mph	o	4-minute pitstop!
	F2	RSM/Kawasaki	25th	24.08	o	
	Classic	P & M/Honda	22nd	21.49 = 103.7 mph	Bronze	102.35 mph ave.
1984	F1	VF750 Honda	N/S	—	o	Chain tensioner
	Senior	P & M/Honda	Rtd	21.46 = 103.9 mph (practice)	o	Lap 1 – points!
	Historic	RSM/Triumph	4th	25.002 = 90.5 mph (s/s lap 1)	Silver	£150 – rained
1985	F1	Press road-	29th	21.37 = 104.6 mph	o	Fastest lap!
	Prod	test 750	21st	22.15 = 102 mph	o	Wet lap 1
	Senior	,,	35th	22.09 = 102.1 mph	o	
1986	F1	Press GSX-R	58th	21.54 = 103 mph	o	Wet & foggy
	Prod 750	,,	42nd	22.05 = 102 mph	o	Showers!
	Prod A	GSX-R 1100	18th	21.21 = 106 mph	o	Fastest laps yet!
	Senior	P & M/Honda	Rtd	—	o	Three cylinders
1987	F2	Harris/Honda	29th	22.19 = 101.5 mph	o	Prod bike, two stops
	Senior	GSX-R	Rtd	21.28	o	Very wet!

Prod A and C cancelled due to bad weather.

Year		Machine	Result	F/laps	Replica	Remarks
1988	Prod C	Harris/Honda	25th	104+ mph	o	Broke lap record! (it was broken 73 times)
	Prod A	Suzuki	26th	108 mph	o	
	Junior (F2)	Honda	27th	105 mph	o	Petrol tap last lap (no reserve!)
	Senior	Suzuki	30th	20.44 = 109.1 mph	o	Fastest yet!

Year		Machine	Result	F/laps	Replica	Remarks
1989	Senior	600 Honda	37th	102 mph ave	o	
	Prod A	GSX-R	N/S	—	o	Engine knock
	F1	Kawasaki	36th	103 mph	o	Proddy bike
	Prod B	,,	Rtd	104 mph	o	Petrol ran out!
	600 S	Honda	26th	103 mph ave	o	
1990	600 S	600 Honda	23rd	101 mph ave.	o	Wet last lap
	400 S	400 Honda	20th	98 mph ave.	o	£30 prize money

Summary to 1990:
80 races entered
24 retirements
 2 non-starts
 2 cancellations
17 replicas
Approximately 25,000 miles covered

The Suzuki GSX-R 1100 achieved a lap of 20.44 mins—109 mph

22 Principal names of the course

One of my own particular methods of learning the course, many years ago, was to memorize the names of its features. Given any name by a friend, the game would be to remember the names immediately before it and after.

The principal corners have signposts that give an indication of the sort of bend to come, and these stick in the mind quickly. Calling to mind the names of the corners before and after soon fixes the shape of them in the mind, too, and soon the sections will start to blend together.

Going to the Island for the first time with this *aide-mémoire* can save some valuable time. From reading the course notes, make a notation of 'right' or 'left', 'fast' or 'slow' against the following names if you can.

St Ninian's crossroads	Sarah's Cottage	Sulby Bridge	Verandah
Bray Hill	Creg Willys Hill	Ginger Hall	Les Graham Memorial
Quarter Bridge	Lambfell	Kerrowmoar	Bungalow
Braddan Bridge	Cronk-y-Voddy	Glen Duff	Hailwood Heights
Snugborough	Drinkwater's Bend	Glentramman	Brandywell
Union Mills	Handley's Corner	Churchtown	The Thirty-Second
Glen Vine	Barregarrow crossroads	Milntown Cottage	Windy Corner
Crosby village	Barregarrow	Schoolhouse	The Thirty-Third
Crosby crossroads	The Thirteenth	Parliament Square	Keppel Gate
Highlander	Kirk Michael	May Hill	Kate's Cottage
Greeba Castle	Rhencullen	Cruikshanks	Creg-ny-Baa
Appledene	Bishop's Court	Stella Maris	Brandish
Greeba Bridge	Alpine Cottage	Ramsey Hairpin	Hillberry
Ballacraine	Ballaugh	Waterworks	Cronk-ny-Mona
Ballaspur	Ballacrye Rise	Tower Bends	Signpost
Ballig	Wildlife Park	Gooseneck	Bedstead
Doran's Bend	Quarry Bends	Guthrie's Memorial	The Nook
Laurel Bank	Sulby crossroads	Mountain Mile	Governor's Bridge
Black Dub	Sulby Straight	Mountain Box	Glencrutchery Road
Glen Helen	Sulby village	Black Hut	Start/finish

Bibliography

Racing and Tuning Production Motorcycles (Speed & Sports Publications, May 1970)
How to Start Production Motorcycle Racing (Speedsport Motorbooks, March 1973)
TT Racing (Speedsport Motorbooks, 1974)
Road Bike Racing & Preparation (Osprey Publishing, 1989)